AFTER RAIN
SHINES THE SUN

After Rain
Shines the Sun

Brigitte Schalke

To order additional copies of this book, contact:
Xlibris Corporation
1-888-795-4274
www.Xlibris.com
Orders@Xlibris.com
38706

CONTENTS

BIOGRAPHY

My name is Brigitte Schalke. I was born on July 23, 1940 in Germany in the city of Zoppot, county of the free city of Danzig. After I was born my birthmother abandoned me and luckily my Grandma who I called Mama raised me. At that time it was World War II in Germany. We faced starvation, fear and running for our lives. Fortunately we survived this nightmare although more pain and suffering took place for years to come. In 1947 we had to leave the northern part of Germany, located at the East Sea. We were forced onto a cattle car on which we lived for three weeks under inhuman conditions; cold, filthy and hungry. It was a ride to the unknown. We arrived at a small village in the southern part of Germany that became our new home.

We worked hard on a farm to fill our hungry stomachs. In 1949 Germany was divided into two parts, East and West. Unfortunately we lived in East Germany that had a negative effect on us for many years.

In 1950 my Grandpa arrived and that was the beginning of another nightmare. He raped me consistently until I was 14 years old. My Mama and I were abused and tortured by him on a daily basis. Years later he passed away but the damage was done for the both of us. Mama became very ill and left me forever when I was 26 years old. I never got over that loss and to heal myself I decided to have a baby, which became another painful experience because I almost lost him.

My son, Michael, was born in 1972. The first year of his life was very difficult for him; he suffered from a hole in his stomach but fully recovered and went on to a successful life.

After two years of negotiations by the American Ambassador in Berlin Mike and I were allowed to leave East Germany. I owe this To President Jimmy Carter. My stepfather had written to him and he instructed the

Ambassador to help us; and indeed he did! The American Government traded computers to the East German Government for Mike and me and in 1977 we left the Communist country and joyfully entered freedom in West Germany.

In June 1977 we came to the United States and settled in Southern California where we live to this day. I learned English, Mike graduated from Cal State Northridge and perhaps most importantly; I became a U.S. citizen in 1984.

After many years of painful memories of my childhood and life in East Germany I've come to grips with them and finally got enough courage to face them and write this book. During the months of tears and pain of writing it I came to the conclusion that *AFTER RAIN SHINES THE SUN.*

CHAPTER I

Sunrise

The sound of sweet melodies woke me up on that Saturday morning, and I felt like the birds were singing just for me. How beautiful it was to start a new day and I was looking forward to seeing more sunshine because my son was coming to visit.

"Happy birthday Mom, today I will take you to your favorite place. I knew this must be the beach." As we arrived my son had a big present for me. "Open it Mom, I hope you like it."

"I couldn't figure out what my surprise was until I unwrapped it, a pretty picnic basket full of all kinds of goodies. How nice Michael, I like it very much, thank you. You sure come up with some nice ideas and know how to surprise your Mom, that's very lovely."

"Remember Mom, how many times we have been to this beach?"

"Yes Michael, I remember watching you surf almost every weekend since you were 12 years old."

"Why do you like the ocean so much Mom?"

"Maybe because I was born by the sea."

"Mom, you always told me about your Mama, how she raised you and how much you loved her, but you never talk much about the rest of your life."

"You're right son, there were times in my life that made me sad, they were difficult to talk about, but you have a right to know and I will tell you how it used to be."

THE GRAND HOTEL

The City We Called Home

It's summer time in a city at the sea. The sky is clear and blue, people are sitting in the cafes and restaurants, walking on the pier and gambling in the big Grand Hotel and Casino overlooking the beach. Kids are playing in the white sand and warm water. It's such a peaceful place to be, it's a paradise. Zoppot, the city we called home, was very famous. My Mama told me she saw the Kaiser Family, the Fuehrer, movie stars, and many other rich and famous people. Sometimes the Hindenburg and Graf Zeppelin would fly over the city. People came not only from Germany, but also from all over Europe to vacation there. When Mama was young and had just married, she worked in the Grand Hotel as a masseuse and gave the guests mud baths. Her husband had a job at the roulette table and if somebody was a big winner he came home in the morning drunk.

But all the peace and beauty of this picture will suddenly change over night. It is the year 1940 and World War II in Germany. Large clouds of smoke, fire, and ashes cover the city, while buildings are falling like matchsticks. During this time an innocent baby girl is born. This little one was me and this is where my story begins.

Please be my special guest, sit down, relax and allow me to tell you my life story.

Mama

After I was born my birthmother rejected me. She was very young and did not want the responsibility of raising a young child. In those days this brought shame to our family, and people would always point fingers at us. I was a very lucky baby, because my grandma tucked me under her wings. My birthmother disappeared and I didn't see her for many years. The only woman in my life was my grandma, loving and caring for me. I called her Mama because that's what she was to me. She gave me the name Brigitte but called me Gittchen. Her name was Lucie and her husbands' Karl. Together they had two children, my birthmother Christel and her brother Fritz. He was only 16 years old when he had to go to war; he never came back. He was killed in action. Her husband Karl was also in the war but nobody knew where or even if he was still alive. My biological father served the Fatherland in the Navy on a destroyer. He was killed in Norway at the young age of 20, two months before I was born. The only memories I have of him are a picture in his Navy uniform and his death certificate, discolored with holes and burn marks. Two of my Mama's brothers were also killed. Leo, the older one, was on the Russian front in the bitter, cold winter. He came home alive but his leg up to the knee was frostbitten. It turned black and had to be amputated. Some years later he died from complications.

There was nobody around us anymore! It was only my Mama and me; we were the only ones left. She took me in her arms, holding me very tight and said, "It's just the two of us, and you and I are family." My Mama was very

MY BIOLOGICAL FATHER

MY BIRTHMOTHER DISAPPEARED

THIS WAS THE LAST TIME I SAW MY UNCLE FRITZ

ONLY 16, HE HAD TO GO TO WAR

special; I admired her, loved her, and looked up to her. By her side I felt safe, she represented many people to me. She was my Mother, Father, Brother, Sister and my best friend. Mama was my everything, sweet and wonderful! She must have been in so much pain, her pretty face looked tired with tears in her blue eyes.

My First Nightmare

I must have been about four years old when the nightmare started, a nightmare that I would never forget for the rest of my life. The house we lived in was two stories, with a big back yard and rosebushes in the front. It was located in a nice neighborhood one block from the beach.

All the young men are at war, only the elderly, the sick and mothers with little children are left behind. They are scared and my Mama lets some of the neighbors stay in our house to give them shelter. We kids were lying on the bed like sardines in a can. The mothers are on the floor, always on alert. What happened next was a nightmare for all of us and I still see it like it was yesterday.

It's late and time to sleep, at least for the kids. All of a sudden I heard a big noise. I saw three soldiers with flashlights, smashing the door with their machineguns. Everybody started screaming as they stormed into the house. The soldiers began to tackle the women and rape them in front of their children and babies. Imagine the women screaming and fighting while we kids were all crying. It was a horrible scene and a nightmare. During the struggle, my Mama somehow escaped the house and yelled for help. After a while she came back with another man in a different uniform. I remember how angry he was as he commanded them to follow him outside. We never found out what happened to those three soldiers, I just hope they paid a price for what they did.

One day my Mama said to me, "Gittchen we are going to have to dig a hole in the front yard and I want you to help me." As little as I was I wondered what all this was about, and I would find out very soon. Mama put jewelry and some important papers in a bag. After we began to dig for a while, she lay the bag in the hole. She said "Let's cover it very neatly so nobody else can see it and we will come back for it later." But at the time we had no idea that we would never see it again.

I was always hungry and my stomach hurt so much. I remember after dark we went behind the rich people's villas, the ones still standing and not leveled to the ground. We picked through the dumpsters for food. Sometimes we got lucky and found some half rotten food, but we did not complain and ate it. There were days where we did not have anything to eat, so we ate grass, mud, chicken poop, anything that would quiet our stomachs. We would even drink water from the street storm drains in order to survive. Even at my age, I learned how painful hunger could be. Sometimes the hunger was so intense that I would become unconscious and other times become hysterical and start to lose my mind.

Mama found a job as a housekeeper, which was good because it gave us something to eat. She never let me out of her sight even when she was working. I remember sitting in the corner on the floor drawing pictures and watching Mama. One day she forgot something and we went back to the house. "Gittchen," she said, "you wait on the steps for me and I will be right back."

Being the good kid that I was, I said, "Ja, Mama," and did what she told me to do. After waiting awhile, I heard yelling and screaming, and as I looked up, I saw Mama running towards me crying. A man chased after her beating her with a large stick. She collapsed right in front of me, covered with blood. I was so scared, and as I cried I laid my little body over her. I yelled, "Mama, Mama, please don't die and leave me alone."

Seeing the big, open wound on her head and all the blood pouring out, I became hysterical. Shortly after, neighbors came to help and covered her head with a towel. Later I found out why Mama's boss was so upset: my birthmother had an affair with him but Mama knew nothing about it. When he asked Mama where her daughter was, she told him she did not know because she had not seen her for a long time. He called Mama a liar and started to beat her. What if I lost Mama that day? How would my life be without her? A little girl all alone in this big dangerous world! But thank God my Mama survived the beating and we were still together.

I will never forget the horrible things I had to witness as a young child, especially the terror and fear. Every city was a target, and when we heard the loud sirens, it was a warning that the bombers were on their way. Shortly after, we heard lots of them coming closer. I never forgot the sound, getting louder and louder. Mama took me by her hand and we ran for our lives. We tried to make it to the bunker down the street or into the basement of a building. The airplanes were right above us. As the bombs started to fall we hit the ground and froze. All around us there were explosions, fire, smoke, and collapsing buildings. We did not have any place to run, and death was waiting for us everywhere. I could hear people screaming and moaning, and I saw dead bodies and their parts all around. Many of them were charred, burned, and still smoking. The scene and smell was horrible. I was terrified, scared and crying. It was too much for a little girl, too much for everyone. Mama was holding me very tightly. She covered my eyes and said, "Don't look."

But it was impossible not to see, because it was happening all around us. My eyes were burning from all the smoke, my throat was hurting, and my feet felt like they were on fire. I heard babies crying for their mothers, the wounded and the dead, and mothers calling for their children. I will never forget how a mother was holding her baby screaming her heart out as she yelled, "My baby, my baby, somebody help me!"

This happened right in front of us. Mama ran for help, but it was too late for the little one. It was lifeless in her mother's arms. To see the faces of the dead, the horror and fear in their wide-open eyes, was something that no one should have to face or remember in life. There are no words to describe this nightmare, and it seemed like the world had come to an end. Somehow we survived, but would we be as lucky tomorrow?

Sometimes the airplanes would attack at night. When the sirens howled and all the lights went out and the city went pitch dark, we started fearfully to run for shelter again. We had never run so much as we did then. Sometimes we would make it to the bunker, but it was so overcrowded that there wasn't enough room for so many people. Only if someone died could they make room for another to squeeze in. Even after the planes disappeared, we knew they would come back. Everywhere I saw tanks and soldiers, bullets flying through the air, and in the blink of an eye we could be shot or blown up. It was very scary, no matter where we turned. Bombs fell from the sky, bullets on the ground and ships shelling us from the sea. I was just an innocent little child but found myself in the middle of hell.

Sometimes the attacks would occur without warning. I can remember one day, when we ran to the nearest house for cover. Just as we entered the house a bomb hit it. The walls and ceilings collapsed, smoke, fire, and debris was all around us. I couldn't see or breathe and I cried out for Mama.

"I am over here," she screamed. "I think I'm all right."

The next thing I remember, someone put a gas mask on my face. It was a soldier, and he moved us outside as we watched the burning house collapse in ashes. Covered in debris, with cuts all over, and badly shaken, we survived, thanks to the help of the Unknown Soldier. This was a very close call. We didn't know where that young man came from or who he was, but one thing we did know was that he was our guardian angel because he saved our lives that day. He disappeared into the smoke and we never had a chance to thank him.

We prayed everyday for this nightmare to come to an end and begged for mercy. But God didn't hear us. I don't know where we got our energy from, since we never had anything to eat and were always on the run. And Mama was always worrying about me. So many times she risked her life in order to protect me from being hurt. She never complained, and no matter how difficult a situation was, she kept going on, and always found a way out. We had been running for our lives for days, weeks, and months. No matter where we went there was no way to escape or a safe place to be. But fortunately, we were still alive and we had each other.

In those horrible times, peoples' lives were turned upside down from all the pain, frustration, and loss of their loved ones. So many innocent people were killed. Families were torn apart and destroyed. So many broken hearts and wounds so deep, some would never heal. I was too little to understand why all this happened, but I was there, it was real and very painful. Living through this entire trauma was damaging for my small and fragile body. I was always depressed and would cry very easily. I would not talk much and did not trust anyone. Every loud noise would make me jump and tremble. I lived in a shell and could not get out of it. I was depressed for many years.

One day Mama said to me, "Gittchen, let's go and see if our house is still OK." When we arrived, all we could see was a giant pile of rubble that used to be our home. The digging we did some time ago was all for nothing. We had no home and no jewelry; everything was gone. As we looked around, it was so painful to see how such a beautiful city became an ugly ghost town. It was unbelievable, like a bad dream.

How could such a horrible thing happen? Millions of innocent people lost their lives, and all of Europe had suffered, but as Germans, we paid a very high price. The war in Europe lasted five years, eight months and six days. Germany lost 2.85 million soldiers and half a million civilians. And why? For greed, power and hatred. How was it possible that one human mind could create such a nightmare?

The Nightmare Ends

Time went by and we survived the unthinkable. I am a big girl now almost 5 years old. One day it was silent, no more airplanes, no more shooting. It was strange for us, and something we were not used to. The next moment I saw people jumping, dancing, yelling and hugging each other. The tanks stopped, soldiers dropped their guns and ran. I didn't know what was going on until Mama threw me in the air and shouted

"Thank God, Thank God, it's all over, it's all over." We cried tears of joy. This was May 7th, 1945, the end of the War and the end of a nightmare. How we survived this nobody knew! It was a miracle!

Now we saw better days to come, all the suffering came to an end, but there was still more crisis on the way, waiting for us. Living in peace and without pain was not meant to be for the two of us. We were in bad shape, dirty, smelly, weak, clothes torn apart, shoes with big holes in them, and like always we were hungry. We were exposed to rain and snow, slept on the street or in bombed out buildings. I will never forget this horrible time of my life and how we searched for the strength to go on.

Leaving the Destroyed city

We didn't know what to do or where to go. The house was gone the city was destroyed. Everyone that survived left, with nothing or a few belongings. Mama decided that we would go to stay with her sister who was living on a farm. "If we are lucky and they are still alive" she said, "we will have food, milk, and a roof over our heads." So we started walking. At that time I had no more shoes, my feet had open wounds and were bleeding. Every step was torture and I cried from the pain. Mama ripped the bottom of her skirt off and used it to tie around my feet. Once in a while she carried me in her arms. It seems like there was no end to the sandy road, and we moved slower and slower. "Hang on Gittchen" Mama said, "We will be there soon." After a while she yelled, "There it is! I can see it." What a relief it was, because I didn't know how much longer I could go on. This was the first time I was out of my home city, and I did not know what to expect living on a farm.

The first person we saw was Mamas' sister Anna, she looked just like her. The two fell into each other's arms and cried. What a surprise she said, "I thought you two were dead; it's nice to see you two alive." Then the rest of the family came to welcome us. She had two daughters Lena and Anka, with blond curly hair, and blue eyes. Both the girls looked so fresh with their red cheeks like a flower in the spring. Her husband Joseph welcomed us too. He had a bad leg and was dismissed from the war. Felix, their oldest child, was on the war front somewhere but had never returned. He was killed at the age of 21. And there was another family member named "Bruno," a beautiful German Shepard. We soon became best friends. This was the first time I met all of Mama's family, and I liked them all. Now we were able to take care of ourselves. We were able to bathe and wear fresh clothes. I got mine from the girls, they were much too big but I didn't care because Mama would fix them later. It felt so good to be clean after such a long time. We must have looked like Gypsies, but now we were civilized. I didn't know what I wanted more, to eat or take care of my bloody and burned feet. The whole family took good care of our needs. Finally we found people who cared for us and treated us like human beings. I hadn't eaten so well in my whole life. My stomach was not used to it and rejected everything. But after some time it got better and my feet began to heal.

Now the air was clear, I could see the sun, the blue sky, the moon, stars, and smell the flowers and grass. There was no more dead body stench. I could hear the birds singing, because there was no sound of sirens, airplanes or exploding bombs. At night everybody sat by candlelight and listened to Mama's stories. Shy like I was, I sat in the corner with Bruno by my side. Many questions had been asked but there were so few answers.

Life on the Farm

The farm was nice with lots of land around and close to the sea. There were many animals, fruit trees, berry bushes, and even a private forest. The house was one story and had a roof that was made of straw. To me it felt like I was in paradise. I could eat as much as I wanted and drink fresh milk everyday. What a treat it was after all of the starvation. Sometimes we took a small boat to the sea and went fishing. One day, I remembered that we caught crabs, and that's what we were having for dinner. There were three or four of them crawling on the kitchen floor. Mama and her sister put a big pot on the stove to boil water. I was lying on the floor pointing my finger at the crab, when it snapped at my hand almost cutting off my finger. I was bleeding and crying, I should have left the crab alone. They were dropped alive into the boiling water, I could hear the noise they were making like they were in pain and then they turned red. To see them cooked alive and suffer, I couldn't eat dinner that night.

Life on the farm was very simple in those days, but there was lots of hard work that came with it. Everybody had to help and so did I. There were many things that I learned to do, like feeding the animals, cleaning up and working in the fields. I always like being around the animals. There was no electricity or running water. We got our water from an outside pump and well. We hand carried the water bucket into the house for our needs. The toilet was an outhouse. The clothes were washed by hand with a washing board. Everything was laid out on the grass to dry. The sheets had to be ironed and neatly folded. The iron was big and heavy; the lid on top would be opened hot charcoal would be place inside it.

There were lots of storks around the farm. On the roof of the house every year they would build a nest for their chicks on a big wagon wheel that was tied. For me it was so fascinating, that I could sit there for hours and watch. Then one day I saw the little chicks, how the mother and father storks fed them and taught them to fly.

And how could I forget the turkey attack? One day we visited a neighbor. As we were leaving, a turkey came after me, and suddenly jumped on my back and attacked me. The farmer chased him away with a broomstick. I didn't know why this big bird attacked me. Maybe it was the red sweater I was wearing that day. He hurt me but I was okay, just a little shaken up.

In the summer I ran around barefoot most of the time, and like always I played with Bruno. Suddenly, I felt a sharp pain in my right foot. I cried out loud for Mama. She came with her sister to see what was the matter. A big rusty nail was stuck in my foot. The moment Mama pulled it out, blood was shooting all over like a fountain. The wound became infected and took a long time to heal. No more running around for a while until my foot healed.

But after all, life on the farm was fun, and slowly we started to recover from all our pain and suffering. The winter was very cold with lots of snow and there wasn't much to do outside. We spent a lot of time inside the house around the warm oven. The women spun the wool from the sheep and later made sweaters, socks, hats and gloves. Joseph, I called him Uncle, was busy cutting tobacco stems, and scrambling the leaves for his cigarettes and pipe. The plants grew behind the house, and after they were ready to harvest, we cut them, bundled them, and hung them to dry. I liked to help Uncle Joseph, and he appreciated it. Everything was done by candlelight or petroleum lamp. Sometimes it snowed so hard that the day turned into night. The house was snowed in; the only way out was to dig a tunnel from the inside out. There was always a shovel behind the door just in case.

For me wintertime was lots of fun; building a snowman in front of the house, it was always bigger than me or making snow angels and having a snowball fight. I got my first pair of snow skis and learned how to ice skate. This was the first time in my life that I had fun and could enjoy being a kid. Every Sunday we all went to church in the village nearby. There was a big snow sled on the farm. Uncle Joseph would put a leather harness with a bell on the horse, and off we went. I was always so excited to go, not to church, but just for the sled ride. And how much fun I had, sitting "on top of the world", cuddled in blankets and breathing the crisp fresh air. Sometimes the sled would flip over and everyone would fall into the deep snow. We started to catch up on all the things we had been missing for years before, but now life was good. But soon there would be another crisis around the corner, waiting for us.

Something was in the air I could feel it. Everybody stuck their heads together whispering and I saw Mama crying again. This was not a good sign and I started to worry. "Come to me Gittchen, I need to talk to you." After looking in her face, I knew at that moment that this must be bad news. She said, "You have to go to school and learn Polish."

I was confused and didn't understand. We spoke German, why did I have to learn Polish? The first day Mama came along, and after that I was on my own. The school was in the same village where we went to church; it must have been the only one around. I didn't like it but went everyday. Almost everyday I was scared to death because airplanes flew overhead at a very low altitude. I did what I used to, I fell to the ground and froze. But to my surprise they never dropped bombs or shot at me. I was very uncomfortable with the situation, and told Mama about it.

"It's okay Gittchen, don't be scared they will not hurt you anymore." Everyday I cried and begged Mama, please don't make me go but she said, "I'm sorry Gittchen but you have to. I knew she was the last person on earth who would want to see me unhappy or scared.

One day I came home and Mama said, "Gittchen, I have good news for you. Today was your last day of school." First I had to go and now I didn't, all my confusion started all over again. I was relieved and happy and didn't even ask why, even after going to Polish school for six months. Although I didn't like it, I was able to speak two languages, one fluently and the other okay. But something didn't seem to be right, and as hard as I tried, I couldn't figure it out.

I liked not going to school anymore. Now it was time for me to catch up on things; playing with Bruno and helping out around the house or outside. One day a lady I had never seen before came to visit. She baked cookies and made coffee. I was hanging around and watching her. After a while she asked, "Would you do me a favor?"

"Yes madam I would like to" I answered, and stood by her side. I wanted to help; it made me feel good that someone needed a little girl like me. She gave me a big can of hot coffee and a basket of cookies and said "Please take this to the people in the field." I remembered that Mama let me wear a new sweater that day, with different colors she made for me. I went on my way but had a problem with the big can because it was heavy. The field was uphill and I could see everyone. Somebody yelled, "Look little Gittchen is bringing us something." Somehow I tripped and fell, the lid from the can opened and all the hot coffee poured over my left arm. I cried and screamed, it hurt so much. Mama and her sister carried me to the house. The moment my sweater was removed I screamed loudly from the pain. All the skin was stuck to the inside of the sleeve, and all I saw was bloody flesh. I felt sick and began to vomit. Immediately, I was taken by a horse drawn wagon to the nearest doctor. "Oh my god" he said, "This does not look good." I had never felt this much pain before; it was like somebody ripped my arm off! After the doctor treated me, my arm was in a big bandage and hurt like hell. I would carry that pain with me for a long time. "It's all my fault," the lady said, but I wasn't mad at her, to me it was an accident.

An official letter came; Mama read it and began to cry. From times before, I knew it was something bad, and how right I was. We had two options; stay and become Polish, or leave and not be allowed to return. Never before had I seen Mama so angry, her whole body was shaking, and she was yelling, "I was born as a German and I will die as a German. I never harmed anyone, why can't we be left alone and live in peace?" I will never forget her words.

German areas where we lived had been captured by the Polish and Russian military and been claimed as Poland. This is why there was all the confusion about me going to a Polish school and why we decided to leave. Life on the farm was good and we had just started to recover. Our health improved and our bodies got stronger. But now there was a new problem we had to face. Happiness was not meant to be for us, and another nightmare was about to take place.

CHAPTER II

My First Train Ride

P eople make many decisions in their life, some for good and some for bad. Mama decided we should leave. "With all we have been through, we will survive this one too." She put some important documents like birth certificates and a few photos in a bag. The day came to say goodbye. I remembered that it started to snow again. It was very heartbreaking for all of us, a very sad day with lots of tears. Finally we had a family and people who cared for us, but we had to go. I took Bruno in my arms and cried. He must have felt something because he looked so very sad. His tail was always wagging when he saw me, but not on that day. Now it was time for us to go, wearing our only clothes and Mama holding my hand, it was time for us to leave. Just like two years earlier, we were walking on the sandy road again, only this time it was in a different direction to the train station. Once in a while we turned around to see the ones we left behind, and how quickly they disappeared from our sight.

Every kid's dream was to ride on a train. For me it was my first time and I was very excited, but shortly I found out what a horrible experience it would become. After a long walk from the farm we arrived at the train station. My idea of a train was different from what I saw. It was a cattle train waiting for us with lots of people standing around, both young and old. "Was this the train I will have my first ride on?" I asked myself. Men in uniform pushed everyone inside the cattle cars and yelled "schnell, schnell." Nothing on the floors, no food, drinks, or bathrooms, so many people, so little room. We all sat close together which kept us a little warm. I didn't see any expression on their faces; only sadness and fear in their eyes. Some people asked a man in uniform, "Where are we going?" With a smile on his face he answered, "All of you are going for a fun ride!" I had a bad feeling and knew we were not going to wonderland.

The train was very long and as I heard the big doors closing it started to move. Many people were sick, babies were crying from hunger and the cold. I was not in good condition myself, my arm was still hurting and my bandage was soaked in blood. I remember the old man who sat next to me; he died later that same day. Some people relieved themselves; the smell was horrible, we lived in cruel conditions. Once a day the train stopped at a station. The first thing Mama did was take me to the Red Cross to treat my arm. It was very painful but I knew it had to be taken care of. We would stay in long lines for warm tea and soup. At least that's what they called it, more like warm water and tea. We didn't complain, everything warm in our stomachs felt good.

We had to hurry. After awhile the train started to roll again. I never forgot the day when the train stopped in the middle of a field covered with heavy snow. Some people jumped off to take care of their needs. A lady went further behind some bushes. The train started to move faster and faster, her arms rose over her head she yelled, "Wait for me, please wait for me." The deep snow stopped her from running towards the train. She was left behind and we never saw her again. A little boy about my age was crying for his mother, left behind and all alone. We all watched this happen, powerless to help. It was heartbreaking. Mama comforted the boy until we arrived at the next train stop, and gave him to the nurse at the Red Cross. We never found out if those two were ever reunited. The train ride was a horrible experience, we felt like animals and smelled like them too.

After about three weeks of living on the train, it stopped at another station. I remember it was dark, very cold and snowing hard. Somebody called our names to step outside. "That's it," a man in uniform said, "No more train ride for you two." He pointed with his hand for us to go behind the building, "there is somebody waiting for you." We looked at each other and didn't know what to say. The moment I saw Mama's distressed face, she looked like she was crying out for help. We went where the man told us to go, and I saw a man standing next to a wagon and horse. "I'm here to pick you up and take you to my house," he said. Mama didn't trust the stranger. Not saying anything she took my hand and we went back. The train was gone but the man in uniform was still standing around. Mama started asking questions and after some arguing he said, "It's okay lady, you and your child will have a new home." I think Mama was tired of being pushed around, so we went back to the strange man with the wagon.

"Where are we?" Mama asked.

"Dannheim, in the southern part of Germany," he answered.

Mama took a deep breath of relief and said, "Thank god, I was afraid we were in a different country, but this is still my homeland." That day was the 10th of November 1947; I was seven years old. My dream of riding on a train came to an end and what a ride it was.

Our New Home

After riding in the wagon for some time, we arrived in a small village called Dannheim. The farmer introduced us to his wife, and took us up some creaky old wooden stairs. The farmer's wife opened a door to a very small room. There was an old sofa, small table, two broken chairs, a blanket and a small iron oven with a pot on top. "We hope you two will be comfortable," they said. After they left, we just looked at each other without saying a word. The farmer's wife came back with hot chicken soup and milk, and how we did appreciate it. There was meat and a vegetable in the soup and it was delicious. This was the first good meal we'd had in three weeks. After we finished eating I asked Mama, "Where are we and what will happen to us?"

"I don't know, but don't you worry Gittchen, as long as we have each other we will be okay," she said. Then she took me in her arms and we both cried. After being on the cattle train for so long, it felt like we had just checked into a five star hotel. We were very tired and cold; lying on the sofa felt good but we couldn't sleep that night, it was all too much.

Here we were in a strange place, with nothing, having to start all over again. Why were we always being punished, never finding peace in this world?

The next day the farmer's wife called us into her kitchen and gave us food. I still remember it was meat, potatoes and vegetables. The next day Mama said to me, "Gittchen, let's see if we can get something to eat." We walked from house to house, even to the village nearby. Some farmers gave us an apple, an egg, or a piece of bread; others let their dogs chase us and called us bad names. It was very painful and embarrassing for us. When we returned to the farm couple, Mama asked, "Do you need help on the farm or around the house?" They looked at each other and he said, "Yes we could use some help." He also said "You can live in the house for free and work for food." We didn't want to starve again so Mama said, "It's a deal". We worked hard from sunrise to sunset everyday and in the end we were rewarded with a decent meal. Mama was a proud person and didn't believe in taking from people without giving something back. That's the kind of person she was.

Kids can be very rude, they pointed their fingers at me and laughed. I was the new kid in town and a stranger who spoke differently then they did. Every time I saw them I hid. I never had friends to play with like every other child. Most of them went to school, but I was still working at the farm. It was very hard work, but I never complained and looked forward toward to the end of the day to have a good meal. My little skinny body was always sore and tired, but the next day I would go back to work. My arm started getting better and Mama removed the bandage. Nature is amazing and the human body a wonder, how we are able to heal. I still have some scars, a reminder of the day when I was seven years old.

Living on a farm was a good experience. The farmer couple was surprised at all the things we were able to do, and there was no need to teach us. Mama used to say "What you learn once, you will never forget, and nobody can take it away from you." And she also said, "Everything is easy to do if you know how." She taught me how to bake cookies and make a pie. We made everything from scratch, marmalade from fruit and berries, and we pickled all kinds of vegetables. There were some trees and bushes, we picked the blossoms, dried them and used them for tea. To warm up the room and to cook, we gathered dried branches in the forest. In the wintertime we tied them to a sled to take home. We harvested potatoes, which was not much fun, bending over all day or being on our knees. The good ones went in the basement of the house; the small and damaged ones were used to feed the animals. In those days nobody had a refrigerator. What everyone did to keep the meat fresh was to leave it outside or hang it out the window in the cold. This was a simple solution and a freezer couldn't have done a better job. When I look back now it seems funny but it worked.

One day Mama said to me, "Its time for you to go to school like all the other kids." The first day Mama came along and talked to the teacher, but he was unsure of what to do with me because I had never been to a German school before. I was too old for the first grade so he put me in the second grade. I picked up my studies very fast and learned how to read and write. Slowly I overcame my shyness, the kids became nicer, and I liked going to school. I was anxious for the next day and hungry to learn more, because "knowledge is power" Mama said. I had good grades and the teacher let me skip a grade to a higher level. The school in the village we lived in was too small, only one room in a house next to the church.

Some of the kids had to go to a school in another village nearby and I was one of them. We made a short cut across the fields to get to school, which was about 30 minutes away. There was no kind of transportation during these times. We walked in any weather conditions. In the summer it was not so bad, but in the winter it could be brutal. Most of the time there was so much snow it was impossible to walk. The only way to get to school was to have a pair of skis, and when we arrived we would be wet and cold. The classroom was never heated; our fingers were so stiff that we couldn't hold our pencils. I was sick very often with high fevers and so were the other kids.

During those days, teachers punished students by pulling down their pants and beating them with a stick or ruler, or hitting them with rulers on the fingertips. I was lucky, and never had to experience this. The geography teacher was the meanest one and no one liked him. He had his own technique of punishing students; he would throw a piece of calk at student's faces. Every other week one of the students had a black eye. He hit one boy so hard that he was hospitalized and later lost the vision in one eye. There were a lot of complaints about this teacher before, but after that incident he was dismissed and the beatings stopped. One day the German language teacher said, "We're going to learn another language, how would you like to speak Russian?" I raised my hand and asked, "Can I learn English instead?" The teacher got mad at me and said that we would learn Russian, period!

My handwriting always stood out from the other students and so did my drawing skill. I could sit for hours and draw animals, flowers, and nature and forget the whole world around me. During summer vacation I worked at the farm, while most kids went to camp, on trips with their parents, or just had fun hanging out.

One day, the school director, who was also my math teacher, came by on his motorcycle to the fields looking for me. He asked my Mama if it was okay for me to go to his house and write the report cards for him. I liked when he asked me for several reasons. First, he was my favorite teacher, second, it was an honor for me, and lastly I would know the grades of every student at several schools. Mama was very proud of me and said, "Its okay, she can go." I jumped on the back of his bike and we went to his house. I was writing nicely and neatly, and he gave me a compliment. But the only report card I couldn't fill out was my own. As a reward, I got a sandwich, lemonade and a ride home. Somehow kids found out, but not from me because I kept it a secret. They wanted to give me money, presents or be my friend, to find out what grades they had, but my lips were sealed. I promised the teacher not to tell, and a promise was a promise. For the next several years I had this important job, I was proud, as was Mama. She used to make fun of me and say, "Here comes the teachers' secretary." When the director handed me my report card, I was very happy, I not only had a good grade in his class, but also from the other teachers.

Mama always made sure that I did my homework. My friends often waited outside for me, and I was in a hurry. She checked my papers everyday, and if my work was sloppy, she would make me do it again. I learned very quickly to do it right the first time. On school trips teachers would make us do things that weren't fun at all. We had to pick snails in the wine fields; they were then shipped to France to be eaten in restaurants and hotels as delicacies. We also had to go in the potato fields to pick bugs. The worst was the bloodsuckers, known as leeches. They were brought to hospitals and used for blood treatments. Everything was for a good cause, but all we got was a handful of candies and a sore back.

The farmers' son, Peter, was my age. It was our job to check on the animals after school, because there was always one pregnant. His father told us which one to keep an extra eye on. One day I opened the door of the barn to see how the horse was doing. "Oh my god," I saw two feet hanging out of the mother horse. I was so scared I jumped on my bike and pedaled as fast as I could out to the fields. Out of breath I yelled, "The horse, the horse, the feet are hanging out."

The farmer hurried home on his moped and I followed him on my bike. "Bring me water and towels Gittchen, hurry, hurry."

As I watched I thought, if this baby falls, it will get hurt, because it's a long way to the ground. Shortly after it dropped, it tried to stand. I helped the farmer clean up the baby horse, which would always try to stand up but kept falling down. It was a girl; she was cute and had long shaky legs. "Gittchen," the farmer said, "You helped me bring this baby into this world and you can give her a name."

I didn't have to think long and said, "How about Lotti?"

"I like it," he said, "it's a pretty name."

I spent lots of time with Lotti and watched her grow up. Everyday I visited her and made sure she was OK, gave her treats like apples and carrots. Every time I called her name she would turn her head and come towards me. If she was outside running around with her mother and kicking her long legs, she came to me and I would give her a big hug. When I would brush her she looked at me like she wanted to say thanks for taking such good care of me.

If someone could get you in big trouble, Peter was the master. He always came up with some crazy ideas. One day he asked, "Gittchen, would you like to have some fun today?"

"Sure, what did you have in mind?"

"Have you ever seen drunken chickens," he asked?

"No, I haven't."

"Watch me," he said, "I'll show you how."

I was curious because I had never heard of such a thing. He went inside the house and came back with a bottle of vodka, which his father was hiding. He put the chicken feed in a large bowl and poured the vodka over it. All the chickens, about 40 of them, came to eat like there was no tomorrow. I stood back and watched. After a few minutes they all made funny noises, walking like drunks, and one after the other fell to the ground. I was thinking, that's not funny and began to worry. But for Peter it was very funny, and he laughed his head off. I kept my eyes on the chickens but none of them was moving.

At this point I was sure he killed all of them and began to panic. "Peter, Peter, you've killed them. What have you done?"

"He just laughed and said, "Don't worry, they'll all be fine."

How could I believe him seeing all of them lying lifeless on the ground? All of a sudden we heard the farmers moped and we ran behind a pile of firewood to hide. I was scared and thought, oh boy, we are going to be in big trouble. But Peter was still giggling and holding his stomach. As scared as I was, I kept one eye on the farmer and the other on the chickens. I never forgot his face and how he was yelling, "Oh my god, what happened to my chickens?" In his confusion he was running back and forth between the chickens. Finally one after the other came back to life and tried to stand up. It took a while before they all got back on their feet again. What a relief it was for me, I was sure that they were all dead. The farmer was yelling for his son. I didn't blame him for being upset. Peter was grounded for the rest of the week. I was sure that the farmer and I would remember that day for a very long time, not only for the drunken chickens but for the empty vodka bottle as well.

I felt badly and tried to stay away from him but he was not mad at me and said, "I know it was not your idea, you are a good girl." I liked Peter, he was fun to be around, but that day he went too far. I don't know what came over him to get such a crazy idea. The chickens probably had a headache that day but every one of them was ok. The next time Peter asked me to do fun things I was very careful to ask him what he had in mind. Mama didn't like the kind of games we were playing and said to me, "I don't care what Peter is doing, I don't want you to be involved." Even when I was only watching, I felt guilty and promised Mama I would be a good girl. Peter, this little red haired devil with freckles on his nose, almost got me in big trouble.

CHAPTER III

Growing Up

S lowly we got used to our new surroundings and everyday we made a small step forward. It seemed like time stood still in the quiet sleepy town. Everything was done the old fashion primitive way like many years ago. In the town was a mayor whose office was in the same house he lived in; a priest, village policeman, a small fire department, a tiny post office and an even smaller market called Konsum. If you didn't have cash to pay, you could get a loan and pay them back later. Every Wednesday we had to order what we needed and it was delivered by Friday from the city. Every Friday before dusk a man walking through the streets wearing a traditional costume would ring a big bell, greeting the people and sharing news from the village and city for all to hear. He ended his news with a wish for a good nights sleep.

The village people were friendly and the village kids accepted me. It was the first time in my life that I had friends. There was: Doris, she became my best girlfriend, Monica, Christa and Connie. Including the boys, we were always doing kid stuff. Now I had more confidence, nobody pointed fingers or laughed at me. The small village we all called home was ideal. On one side fields and the other side mountains, fruit trees and a pond. All four seasons were beautiful, but my favorite was spring, with all the blossoms and the sweet smells. I enjoyed being in the forest the most. There were so many things to explore, all different kinds of trees, bushes, wild berries and mushrooms. The beautiful colorful wild flowers, so many different birds, each one sang a pretty song.

There were all different kinds of animals: foxes, rabbits, wild pigs, deer, wolves and many more. At night we could hear them howling. I spent lots of time walking in this beautiful place of nature. I drew pictures, studied the wild life and everything around me. After some time I could recognize by name many things in the forest. This became one of my hobbies and paid off in school and later in life.

In the wintertime everything was covered in snow and it was hard for the animals to find food. I helped the ranger many times, bringing hay and nuts for the deer. Often I went alone or with a friend, always some nuts in my pocket. From my own experience I knew what it felt like to be hungry. Feeding the animals was something that I liked to do. I wished that I could save them all, at least I helped a few survive the harsh winter. A deer is a very shy animal, but when they're hungry they come closer to people and houses and the farmers always had some food for them. In the springtime they had babies with white dots all over their bodies. They were so cute with their big brown eyes; I couldn't help but fall in love with them.

In the mushroom season I would go out with a basket and a small knife to pick some. Most of them grew in the ground around pine needles and moss, some on tree trunks. After all of my studies, I was able to tell the difference between good and poisonous ones. (Some looked the same and eating them could be fatal). I remember one family from the village that on Sunday morning went for mushrooms, ate them for dinner and the next morning were found dead, poisoned.

One Sunday Mama came up to me, "Gittchen look what I found." I ran to her, she was standing with a big smile holding a big one, I mean big. The head of the mushroom was bigger than a dinner plate. On the way home everybody came to check it out. Nobody ever saw one that size. I don't know how it spread so fast; somebody came from the local newspaper to take pictures. Mama didn't want to be in the spotlight and asked me if I would like to do it.

"No Mama," I said, "It was you who found the mushroom and I can't take credit for it." The next day Mama made the news, a big picture holding the giant mushroom with a huge smile from one ear to the other, it made her day. After mushrooms get older, little white worms begin to live inside, but Mama got a good one.

Two days later, guess what we had for dinner? Mama fried the mushroom with onions and garlic; it was delicious, but too much to eat for both of us. We shared the rest with the farmers downstairs. On most weekends I went to pick wild strawberries, raspberries or blueberries. Every Sunday we had a fresh pie, made with whipped-cream from egg whites, it was the best desert. Nature gave us so many goodies, we just had to go and pick them. Mama and I were always a team in many ways. To help Mama out, I would tutor some of the village kids and help them with their learning problems. As a reward their parents gave me some eggs, a sausage, vegetables or a little money. I also babysat after school or on the weekends. It made me feel good to be able to give a little bit to help us out.

Winter in the village looked like a wonderland. Trees and bushes covered with snow. Us kids had lots of fun, ice skating on the pond or skiing in the mountains. Often we tied sleds together and raced down the hill, or we tied a harness to the dog to pull us. Some serious snowball fights happened, and some of us got hurt, but that was a part of being a kid and having fun. After the snow melted everything awoke from a long winters sleep. The beautiful flowers, blossoms on the trees and bushes, the animals having babies, and life had begun again with Mother Nature taking care of the rest.

All the kids had bikes except me, I had to watch how much fun all the others had. Outside of the village was a big dumpster on the hill. As often as I could, I went to look for bike parts. Sometimes I found a wheel, a pedal, a seat or even a frame.

Mama didn't like what I was doing and said, "Gittchen, why do you bring all this junk home?"

"I'm building a bike so I can ride with my friends."

She didn't say anything after that she felt bad because she couldn't afford to buy me one. I knew we were poor and it never crossed my mind to ask her for anything. I kept digging in the dumpster and one day I had almost everything I needed. The neighbor gave me some missing parts and helped me assemble the bike. I was cleaning oiling and painting. The only color I had was black, and that was okay with me. Then came the moment for the first test ride. I was very excited.

Mama was watching and said, "Gittchen, be careful and don't go too fast."

Everything worked fine, it wasn't the nicest one but it was mine. I was so proud that day and so was my Mama. Riding up and down the street, I made sure everybody could see me. I yelled, "Look at me, everybody look at me!" What was once somebody's garbage became my treasure.

My First Christmas

As time went by I reached the age of nine. In 1949 Germany was divided, one part East and the other West. Unfortunately, the village we lived in was in the Eastern part; after all, luck was not on our side. It would affect us negatively for many years to come.

For every kid Christmas is a very special time. For me it was to be my first experience of this wonderful time of the year. Mama started baking cookies, made marzipan and all kinds of goodies. It smelled so good in our small place. I liked to help her chop nuts, and afterwards I would lick the bowl. We made angels and stars from paper. On Christmas Eve we went to church. The decorations were so nice and I had never before seen so many candles in one place. A choir sung Christmas songs, the organ played and we all sang together. It was a nice atmosphere and I liked it very much. Mama let me wear my best dress that she made for me, she wore her best clothes and everybody looked very nice. What to wear and not to wear was Mama's decision. I only had one outfit for Sundays and holidays and I wasn't allowed to wear it on weekdays. "That's your good dress," Mama said. I remember my first dress she made for me, it was made of old curtains that the farmer's wife gave to us. It was beige with a flower pattern. When I got a new one, only once a year, I couldn't wait to wear it and show it off; it was so special to me.

After church we went home. It was a peaceful night with snowflakes silently dancing around us and I heard the Angels singing *Stille Nacht, Heilige Nacht*. The moment Mama opened our door, I saw a Christmas tree for the very first time. The candles shined, it was decorated with cookies, stars and angels that we made. My eyes got bigger and bigger, I felt like a kid in a candy store, but this was even better. I was overwhelmed. Shortly after, I heard the heavy steps of someone coming up the stairs. A man with a long white beard, boots and a sack on his back was knocking at our door. Mama must have seen how scared I was and said to me, "It's Santa Claus, he comes to the kids and brings them presents." When he asked me if I was a good girl, I recognized his voice. It was the farmer, but I was still frightened. I had to sing a song or say a poem, and then he opened the sack and gave me presents. I got socks, gloves and sweets.

On Christmas day we were invited downstairs to the farmers' family. They had something I had never seen; a big box that played songs; the Christmas tree stood on top while it slowly rotated. We drank hot chocolate and ate cookies and sang songs. It was the first time Mama and I spent Christmas together quiet and peaceful. The next year there was a Nativity play at church, with real shepherds and live animals. Some of us kids played Angels. Mama made me a long white dress with big wings on the back. I had curly black hair hanging over my shoulders and everybody said what a pretty angel I was, ever the priest gave me a compliment, thanks to my Mama. How could I have missed this wonderful time of year for so long? From then on I was always looking forward to the next Christmas.

CHAPTER IV

Stranger at the Door

A man was standing at our door, a stranger I had not seen before; I remember it was right after my tenth birthday. Mama always told me "Don't talk to people that you don't know." But on that day when the door was opened, he asked for Mama and asked who I was.

"I am Gitta," I answered, "and that's what Mama calls me lately." I liked it better because Gittchen was for little girls. I called, "Mama, somebody wants to see you."

"Who's there?" she asked.

"I don't know, it's a man."

She came to the door and I have never forgotten the look on her face. Her color disappeared, she didn't know whether to laugh or cry. She was in a state of shock, and said, "Karl, what a surprise." She turned to me and said "Gitta, this is my husband." I looked at her and didn't know what she was talking about. He came close to me like he wanted to hug me, but I backed up. I didn't like this man; I saw evil in his eyes! I told Mama how I felt and she said, "This is something new for you, I am sure after some time you will feel better about it." Mama was always right, but not this time. There was lots of talking going on, because they had not seen each other for many years. I don't know if Mama was happy to see him, she never talked about it. But I had the feeling that she was scared and uncomfortable with the whole situation.

The room we lived in was too small for the two of us, so the farmer gave us an additional smaller room, which was helpful. Mama and I went on with our daily lives, while he lay on the sofa all day long doing nothing. We struggled to take care of the two of us and now we had another mouth to feed, which meant working harder. I felt very uncomfortable around him; he was always watching me like he was up to something. From the little money Mama had, he asked her to get cigarettes and beer. I was afraid of him and talked only if he asked me. Besides all that, everything was okay for a while, but soon something else would happen.

My Horrible Nightmare

I will talk about something for the first time ever, which is still very difficult for me after fifty-five years. One day when I came back from school, Karl was lying on the sofa exposing himself. He asked me to touch his private parts. I was so scared, I ran down the stairs and he chased after me. He dragged me into the barn and pushed me down. I screamed, cried, bit, kicked and yelled for help, but he was much stronger and raped and molested me. My whole body was shaking. He hurt me and I was bleeding. I was in such shock; I didn't understand what had just happened to me. Confused, ashamed and feeling dirty, I wanted to disappear into the ground. Mama always taught me the difference between right and wrong but we had never discussed sexual issues. What did I know? I was only a little shy girl from a small village. How was I going to face Mama and tell her? She had gone through so much pain in her life; I didn't want to hurt her more. I decided not to say anything about what had happened to me. Everybody came back from the fields and I just tried to hold back my tears. Everybody will notice, it's written on my forehead I thought, the whole world will notice.

Mama was the only one who asked me, "Are you okay. Gitta, you don't look good, did something happen?"

With a shaky voice I answered, "Everything is okay Mama, don't worry, I'm okay." I lied to her; I wasn't ok and couldn't look her in the eye.

She asked me again, "Are you sure you are ok, you look very disturbed?"

"I'm fine Mama, I'm okay." I lied to her again and felt rotten. I hid my bloody underwear and burned it the next day.

"Let's go inside, its time for dinner soon," Mama said. I was afraid to go inside to see the monster that did this horrible thing to me. He was lying on the sofa with a smile on his face acting like nothing had happened. He kept molesting me and hurting me over and over against my will. "This is a part of being a family and this is our secret. But if you tell anyone I will kill you and your Mama," he said. I believed him because his evil eyes did not lie.

Living in Hell

I remember every Saturday we had soup for lunch, and like always the monster was lying on the sofa watching us. I was afraid to sit down; I would begin to shake fearing what would happen. We worked very hard for what we had on the table, and sometimes he would throw the soup on the floor or out the window. Mama just served the food and we had begun to eat. The moment I looked at him, he took a bowl of hot soup, threw it on my face and yelled, "Why are you looking at me you piece of shit?"

"Mama jumped up and said, "Why are you doing this, the girl was not doing anything?"

"Shut up you bitch," he yelled, and started to throw things around. Mama always gave him the biggest portions just to keep peace, but whatever she did it wasn't good enough and he would find a reason to be mean.

One time Mama put a new vinyl cloth on the table. He had a small cutting board on the table in front of him and was watching us. Whistling a marching song, with a smile on his face, he started to cut the cloth with his knife. He was just waiting for us to say something. Mama and I looked at each other and kept quiet. Many times he took my homework and cut it up with scissors, and destroyed the things we liked. I always loved animals but never had one of my own. On my 11th birthday the farmer gave me a German Shepard puppy. It was a boy and I called him Bruno. What a cute little fur-ball he was; but my happiness only lasted for two weeks. One day I came home from school to find my puppy on the ground dead. He had killed him.

Not one day went by without him yelling, breaking dishes and calling us bad names for no reason. He became violent, beating us with chairs or anything else he could reach. Our rooms were always full of thick smoke. If we tried to open a window, he pushed us away and yelled, "You open them only if I say so!" Our eyes were red and burning and our throats were sore from coughing so much. Many times I did my homework outside to get fresh air.

One day I was on my way upstairs, when I heard yelling and screaming. The moment I opened the door, I saw Mama standing against the wall. He was in front of her, threatening her with a big kitchen knife. We never talked back or fought with him because we knew it would make the whole situation worse. He knew we were scared and it gave him more power. But as I saw Mama in such danger, something happened inside me. I started kicking, biting his hand and scratching his face. He hit me very hard and I flew across the room. I felt something warm running down my chin, and I realized he knocked one of my teeth out. Holding my mouth, I went back to Mama and stood in front of her to protect her; she was trembling and crying. He stood in front of me with eyes like a wild animal, foam around his mouth and shaking while holding the knife against my chest. I knew at that moment that this could be my last breath and I was scared to death. Images flashed threw my mind at that moment, what we had been through, and how many times we almost died. I thought about my Mama standing directly behind me. What if he stabbed me? I couldn't leave Mama alone with him; he would kill her too. I couldn't let this happen, I loved her too much. I don't know what it was, fear, frustration or the instinct of survival; suddenly I started yelling at him.

During this moment I knew I was gambling with my own life. "You monster, you animal, you're crazy you belong in a nut house." He didn't expect somebody to talk back to him, he stepped back, dropped the knife and sat on the sofa. Mama was still shaking and crying, I took her in my arms and said, "Its okay Mama, it's okay."

This was a very close call for both of us. For about one week he was quiet. Then it started all over again. There was no other explanation for me; someone who behaved like this must be crazy and evil. I didn't know, but there must have been a beast inside of him. He had two faces; he told the village people that we were cruel to him and he also told them that we were doing evil things to him. He was the victim, but they didn't believe him.

The next winter was coming soon, and it was predicted to be a very cold one. One night as Mama and I slept, he locked us up. No water, food or going to the outhouse. It was bitterly cold and the bed cover was frozen. The only liquid we had was icicles and snow on the window. That's what we had for breakfast, lunch and dinner. We used a pillowcase as our toilet. We lived in these conditions for over one week. The farmer couple noticed that something was wrong. Mama hadn't gone outside and I didn't go to school. The monster must have been out one day because the farmer and his wife came to see what was going on. They had a spare key, and as they opened the door both yelled at the same time, "Oh my God, what has he done this time? How long have you been in this condition?" They asked us to come downstairs, gave us hot tea and soup and covered us in blankets. We were so cold we couldn't talk and were shivering. The farmer, who was a very quiet man, was very angry and said, "I've had enough of this crazy guy; it's unbelievable what he has done." He waited for the monster to come back and when he opened the door he grabbed him by the neck and yelled "If I see you hurt the girls one more time, I will beat you so badly, you won't know if you are a boy or girl, and I will kick you out of my house."

The farmer must have scared him because it was quiet for two whole weeks, at least until another attack occurred. I was outside when I saw Mama running and yelling for help, he was running after her with an axe.

I ran back to the house, knocked on the door, and yelled, "Somebody come fast because Mama is in danger."

The farmer came with a shotgun, which he used for hunting.

He was very angry and yelled, "If you don't stop now, I am going to shoot, you son of a bitch." I think that did it because he dropped the axe. This stopped him for a while longer, but the torture started again when the farmer was not around. Mama started getting sick, all the abuse was too much for her heart. She went to Doctor Amarell, who was our house doctor. He said to Mama, "Lucy, your heart is not very good, you need rest." This was easy for him to say, he had no idea of what was really happening behind closed doors.

One day I remember very well, it was in Biology class. The teacher asked me to draw a human body on the blackboard. I was good at drawing and happy to help. Suddenly out of nowhere, the farmer appeared and began to whisper into the teacher's ear. Then they turned at the same time and looked at me. My heart almost stopped beating; I dropped the chalk and wondered what might have happened to Mama. The teacher came to me and said, "Gitta, you are dismissed for today. You have to go home, it's your Mama." The farmer left, and I ran home, crying all the way. I was scared. I thought the worst; never sure in what condition I would find my Mama. Maybe she was murdered.

When I opened the door she was crying, shaking and holding her chest. "Gitta, I am glad you are here, please call Dr. Amarell." I panicked seeing her like this and ran down the street to the small post office, and called the doctor for help. (In those days only doctors, lawyers, fireman or police had a telephone.)

"I'll be there as soon as possible," he said, "You stay with your Mama."

The doctor arrived sometime later and walked up the stairs to see Mama. The monster was waiting for him and yelled, "What do you want here? We don't need your help."

"I'm here to see Lucy," the doctor said.

I couldn't believe what happened next, the crazy man pushed the doctor down the stairs, yelling and screaming. "You never come back you hear, I want her to suffer and die."

On his way out, the doctor said, "You are crazy and very sick, you need help." Without seeing Mama, I took him to his car, apologized and asked him for help. Before he left, he handed me a small container of pills and said, "Give some to your Mama and the first thing in the morning and bring her into my office."

I thought, "How can we leave the house, the monster will stop us?" The farmer was my solution so I told him what had happened.

He shook his head and said to me, "Don't worry Gitta, I'll come in the morning and make sure you can take your Mama to the doctor." I was relieved and thanked him for being so kind; we arrived at the doctor's office the next morning without any problems.

"It's your Mamas' heart. She needs rest and must stay away from that crazy man," the doctor told me.

The whole situation was too much for both of us. Mama was ill and I was a nervous wreck. I couldn't concentrate in school; my grades dropped. I was always wondering what would happen when I came home and what we would have to face the next day.

One day when I came home from school, Mama was sitting on the chair crying. I rushed to her, "Mama, was he violent with you today? Did he hurt you?"

"Yes. Please Gitta, help me. I can't see out of my left eye."

I took her to the eye doctor the first thing in the morning. After he examined her he said to me, "Nothing I can do, some blood vessels have been broken." This was a very sad day for both of us; Mama had lost vision in her left eye. She was so unhappy; she couldn't do many things that she liked to do. I felt so bad, not being able to help her. There was one tragedy after another. I never hated anyone in my life, but now I had reached that point. We were frustrated, devastated and didn't know how to stop the violence.

I went to the police and begged for help. "Nothing we can do about it, it's a family matter," they said.

I was angry and asked, "Do you want to wait until someone is killed? If the law can't help us then who can?"

The monster was coughing a lot and went to see a doctor. He was diagnosed with contagious Tuberculosis. People from the Health Department came to disinfect everything in the house and said, "He has to be isolated from my Mama and you," but he refused to go anywhere. The smell of the disinfectant was so strong it made us sick. They also told us to sterilize everything he came in contact with such as plates, clothes, etc. It was easy for them to say. He forced us to use plates and utensils after him without being sterilized. We were frightened, and once a month we had to go and get chest X-rays to make sure we didn't catch the disease. For us it was very embarrassing to go out in public, especially for me. We had bruises all over our bodies, bad cuts that needed stitches and black eyes.

The teacher questioned me about my injuries, and I came up with all sorts of lies, like "I fell down and bumped into something."

Doctor Amarell also asked me; I don't know if he believed me. He said, "You must be very clumsy or you must be a wild child." It wasn't true; in fact I was shy and quiet. I had never told the Doctor about my real situation at this point. Kids made remarks like, "My parents say your Mama's husband is crazy. What did you do to make him beat you up so badly?" They hurt my feelings because they had no idea of what we had to face everyday. How many times did I hide my face, embarrassed, hiding my tears?

Our religion was Catholic, and the day of my communion was getting closer. I remember it was spring, just two months before my twelfth birthday. By going to church with Mama for all these years, I knew it was a big ceremony. She made me a pretty white dress and bought me new white shoes. Two days before, I was riding my bike with my girlfriend Doris. We were being silly and were giggling, when I hit some dirt on the side road. "Bang," we crashed. Doris was okay, but poor me, I slid on my hands, elbow and knees through the dirt. I was hurt and bleeding, and Mama took me to our doctor. He cleaned the wounds and removed the sand and little rocks. My left elbow was the worst and I had a big bandage on it in addition to all of my other bandages. However, pain or no pain, I did not want to miss that big day. The bike was damaged but could be fixed. Thanks to Mama, the dress had long sleeves and covered my arm, the only thing I couldn't do was bend my arm.

Despite limping with pain I was ready for my special day. The church was the biggest one in the city, gothic style, and beautiful inside and out. All the girls dressed in white; the dress, shoes, a long white candle with ribbon and a crown in our hair. I felt like a little princess. All the boys wore black suits; girls sat on the left and boys on the right. All of the kids were a good-looking bunch. This was the highlight of the day, shared by many people. I looked to Mama; she was wearing a nice dress and had a big smile on her pretty face. I know that she was very proud of her little girl. I thanked her for that wonderful day; she had made it possible for me and I told her how much I loved her.

Mama liked to go to church in the city every Sunday. She also liked it when I came along with her. For some time I was on a soccer team. Often on weekends we would have to travel to different places. One Sunday late in the afternoon I came home from a game and noticed that Mama was all exited and smiling.

"How was the game Gitta?" She asked.

"It was fun, nobody lost or won; the score was even."

"You're not going to believe what happened today," she said with a big grin, which I seldom saw. Seeing her face, I knew it must be something good, and she then said, "Today I met a lady in church, and after some conversation I found out she used to live in the same city we came from. What a small world it is!" "She invited us to her house next Sunday after church, would you like to come Gitta?"

"Yes Mama, I will go, that is so strange." I met the lady in church, she was about Mama's age and she was very nice.

"Let's go to my place for coffee and cake and I want you to meet my husband who is blind." He lost his vision from the bombing during the war. I was scared because I had never met a blind person. I was afraid and didn't know how to behave. As she opened the door, a man came with dark glasses and said, "Very nice to meet you please come in." After awhile he came close to me and asked, "Do you mind if I touch your face? This way I can recognize how you look."

"That's okay," I answered. He moved his fingers very softly and carefully over my face and told me how I looked. It was amazing how accurate he was. He moved around the house without hitting anything and told me the exact time on his watch, which had no glass cover on it. I was in awe of this man, but I didn't want to ask him too many questions because I didn't want to hurt his feelings. There was an organ in the corner, and he asked me if I would like him to play. He played wonderfully and I was very touched by it. I found out that he played the organ in big events and at church. He was a professional and very skilled. I couldn't imagine how it must feel not to be able to see, but this man had a positive attitude about life. He always has a smile on his face and something nice to say. He was inspirational to me, and I tried to see the world in a more positive way.

Chapter V

The Way Out

None of the T.B. treatments were doing any good for our protection. The monster often said, "I want both of you to suffer from what I have and die from it."

Next time we went for an X-ray, I told the doctor what was really happening at home and asked for help. He shook his head and said to me, "We can't let this happen, sooner or later both of you will be infected, it's just a matter of time. I am going to order him to check into a special hospital, he can't be around you anymore."

Again it was easier said than done, he refused to go. Shortly after, the Doctor came to our place and told him in a very serious voice, "If you don't go, I will send somebody, and they will make sure you do what I am telling you." He went, but returned after only one week. He dismissed himself without the Doctors permission. He started doing what he knew best, abusing us and raping me, it was like living with a poisonous snake, which could strike at anytime. I couldn't take it anymore, living like this.

"There had to be a way out, there had to be." All of our crying out for help was for nothing. Everybody was afraid of him and we were all alone. There had to be a way to end this violence and my head started to spin around from thinking. I couldn't bear to see my Mama in such pain; she had suffered too much already. I loved her and worried about her health. If I didn't find a way to end this hell, it would kill us. One day, I thought I found the solution. "Mama, why don't you file for a divorce? All the suffering will come to an end, and we could live in peace."

She looked at me and said, "I don't know, a divorce? I'm scared he will kill me! And all the papers and going to court. What will the people think? At my age!"

"Don't worry about the people, they are not married to this bastard, it's your life," I said. "If you let me I will help you with the papers." Finally, after discussing the issue, I convinced her and she said yes. I picked up all the papers she needed and we filled them out together. To make sure they didn't fall into the wrong hands, we did it in the farmers' living room downstairs. Some weeks later, a big envelope addressed to Karl arrived from the courthouse. He looked at it and said, "Court house, this must be a mistake!" After he opened it, he started crying and begged Mama, "Please don't do this to me, I promise to be good and won't hurt you again, I need you."

I knew at that moment he was lying. Mama with her big heart, and fear of him, dropped the charges after his sweet-talking. I could not believe it, we were so close to getting rid of him. "Mama, you're making a big mistake, don't believe a word he says. He won't change," I said. It was quiet for about three weeks, and how right I was, everything started all over again; the abuse, torture and molestations.

But this time Mama was strong and said to me, "Gitta, you are so right, why didn't I listen to you the first time?" Mama was very nervous the day we went to court and so was I. She had witnesses; the farm couple and I told what had been going on, as did some neighbors. To my surprise, Dr. Amarell came and had a story to tell. I think it was payback time for him. In the middle of the hearing the monster started yelling calling us *"whore"* and *"bitch."* This made the Judge very angry and he said, "If you don't behave, I will order you to leave this court." After the last witness was heard, who was Dr. Amarell, justice prevailed and the divorce was granted.

The Judge ordered him to move out and stay away from us. I never revealed the facts about my repeated rapes and molestations. To this day, I have never understood why he wasn't locked up or put into a crazy house. What a relief it was, we were free and did not have to live in horror anymore.

Mama thanked me for helping her through all of this. "Without you Gitta, I would never have had this done, thank you so much." I always wanted to give Mama something back for all that she had done for me. When she needed me the most, I was there for her, only fourteen years old. For me the nightmare finally came to an end, he would never hurt us again. He moved to his sisters up north and died two years later. Our lives were filled with horror and fear for many years, but finally it was over. I was amazed how we survived and were still alive. We were victims of violence, torture, mental cruelty and molestation. Our spirit and hope for a better day to come held us together.

After living through all this I developed a negative perspective towards men. Every time one came close to me, I became a raging bull who saw a red colored flag. I would hiss and wouldn't let any man come close to me. That's how I got the nickname of *Tiger*.

Now we could finally take a deep breath of relief, it was all over. Slowly we started to recover from all the pain, and go on with our lives and live in peace and harmony. Soon after, something else would happen; it would affect me the most. Mama was behaving different lately; I guessed she was still recovering from a state of aftershock. She was always a quiet person, but now she could barely speak and occasionally I would see tears in her eyes.

One day she broke her silence, "Gitta, there is something I have to tell you, but it won't be easy for the both of us. I should have told you this a long time ago, but I couldn't."

I wondered to myself how bad this could be, after all we had been through. "What is it Mama?

She started crying choking and could barely talk and said, "I am not your Mama, I am really your Grandma."

I felt something hit me very hard and yelled, "What are you talking about? You are my Mama and always will be." This news was shocking and painful, how could this be possible? The woman who cared for me and loved me so much was hurting me at the same time. This was unthinkable, it couldn't be true. I was confused, hurt and it seemed like the whole world was collapsing around me. I cried and cried and couldn't stop. The same day after dark, I ran into the woods and hid in a foxhole for two days; no food, water, cold and wet. A German Shepard found me; it belonged to the Ranger who was looking for me. Mama felt very bad and apologized; she didn't know it would hit me so hard. I never got over it but we still loved each other. I kept calling her Mama till the day she left me forever.

A Visitor is Coming

About two months later Mama said to me "Gitta, a visitor coming."

"Who can this be? We don't know anybody".

"It's your Mother," she said. All the confusion started all over again. Now I understood Mama's behavior, she was slowly preparing me for that day. And soon, one day in the afternoon, a strange woman was standing in the doorway, a person who I had never seen before. She looked like she came from a fashion show, lots of make up and jewelry hanging all over her. "I am your Mother," she said, and tried to hug me. But I went to Mama, standing by her side and reaching for her hand.

"It's okay, say hello." I did what Mama said but kept a distance.

"Oh, what a pretty and big girl you are, and what long, black, curly hair you have."

I didn't care what she said, it meant nothing to me and I had no feelings for her because she was just a stranger. For all these years, she hadn't been around and had excuses for everything and worried only about herself. Two days later she left, she disappeared just like she did fourteen years ago when I was born. I was very relieved, because I didn't feel comfortable with her around. She had never been there in all the difficult times, she was never there when I cried or was hurt. Where was she when I needed love? She wasn't by my side on the first day of school, or on my birthday and Christmas. Where was she when I needed her the most? It was my Mama; she was always there for me in good and bad times. We can always pretend, but no one can force us to love somebody.

A neighbor gave Mama an old sewing machine, a Singer. Even though it was difficult for her to see with only one eye, she sewed almost every night, making dresses, skirts and blouses for people. They paid her for doing a good job. She also knit, and taught me how, so I was able to help her. Shortly before Christmas, I could feel the holiday spirit in the air. Everybody was busy shopping and the stores were nicely decorated.

"Gitta, would you like to come with me to the city? I need to buy a few things."

"Yes Mama, I would like to come," I answered. I knew there was always something she would buy for me. We took the bus and off we went. I loved to go window-shopping and see all the nice things and decorations.

"Before we go home," Mama said, "Lets go to Rose Street, they have such nice stores." She stopped in front of a bike store without saying a word. I saw a beautiful new bike, shiny, baby blue and silver in color.

"Look Mama, what a pretty modern bike."

"It sure is a nice one," she said. Somebody had bought it, because it had a sold tag on it. I talked about it all the way home and everyday thereafter. That was my Mama, she had planned this day to make sure I saw that bike and to be certain I liked it. That Christmas, I found the same bike under the tree. It was the nicest present I had ever received, and I was a very happy girl.

I couldn't wait to take it for the first ride, but Mama said, "Take it for a ride tomorrow, Gitta. It's dark and there's too much snow." I was so excited I couldn't sleep, waiting anxiously for the next morning. It was hard to ride because of the snow, but I didn't care.

Everybody checked it out and said, "Wow! What a nice bike you have!" and as proud as I was I replied, "It's a present from my Mama. It's a four speed," (This was something special in those days.) Now I was the kid in town with the nicest bike. My old one started to fall apart, so I took it back to the place where it came from, to the dump on the hill.

My First Job

After I finished grade school, Mama asked me what I wanted to do with my life. "I'd like to see you continue to go to school; it's better for your future. You have good grades and you are a smart girl."

But I had already made plans. I wanted to get a job, earn money and support Mama because she was always poor and worked hard all her life. I wanted to make her life more comfortable and there was another reason. I worried about her health and wanted to stay close to her. We would discuss this from time to time and one day she asked, "What kind of job do you have in mind, Gitta?"

"I don't know." I answered.

"You're very talented, how about becoming an artist?"

"I am not that good Mama, I don't think so." I didn't know what to do with myself, but Mama found the solution.

Some weeks later she showed me an ad in the newspaper, glass engraver needed.

"I don't know if this is something I would like to do." I knew what it was but had no idea how it was done.

Mama said, "Why don't you take all the nice pictures you have drawn and go for an interview?" Mama came with me and after we found the address she said, "I will wait here, this is something you have to do alone." This was a new step in my life, making my own decision and I was very nervous.

After a short conversation, the owner looked at my pictures and asked, "Did you draw these?"

"Yes sir," I answered.

He kept looking and said, "That's very impressive, you have talent. Can you start Monday?"

I was hired on September 3rd, 1955 at the age of 15. It was a small company run by a family. I didn't know what I had gotten myself into, it was so difficult to do, and took me some time before I developed a feeling for it. My teacher was not very nice; he was impatient and yelled all the time. Because of all of that, I was scared and nervous. What he had learned over many years, he expected me to do right the first time. Every day I cried, was frustrated and didn't want to go back.

But Mama cheered me up and said, "No master had fallen from the sky, just be patient and try a little more." The co-workers felt sorry for me and told him, "If you keep yelling at her she will never learn." He stopped yelling so much and would even give me occasional compliment. My confidence grew, and I started to enjoy my work. For three years, I went to a special school and worked in the shop. I graduated with outstanding grades when I was eighteen as a professional glass engraver and designer.

My boss said, "I almost gave up on you from the beginning, but I'm very proud of you. You're are a very talented artist."

"Thank you sir. Believe it or not I almost quit." We both laughed. To do this kind of work you need talent and have to be creative. We all have hidden talents in many ways, I was blessed having this gift and nobody could take it away from me. I never considered myself an artist, for me it was just another job. But many other people had a different opinion about it. If Mama hadn't encouraged me, I don't know what I would have become, maybe I would have been an architect.

I remember how often she would say to me, "Never give up so easily, no matter how hard it is." The day I received my diploma, Mama was very proud of me and my boss had a big smile on his face. I felt proud of my self and thought, "Yes I did it."

My boss took advantage of me by not paying me what he should. I didn't like being used by others, so after five months, I decided to quit. I continued my engraving in the same city in a bigger company with more opportunities and better pay.

To have a bicycle was nice, but I wanted something faster. Having a car was out of the question for someone living in the German Democratic Republic. In order to get a drivers license, you had to be eighteen years old by law. I had to take classes for several weeks, including a driver's simulator. Being the only girl, guys made fun of me and said, "What do you want here? This is for guys only you are in the wrong place." The guys who were the biggest jerks failed the test, but I passed and had the last laugh. This was on my eighteenth birthday, and two weeks later I bought a used scooter, and eight months later a brand new scooter, and the following year a brand new BMW motorcycle. I was the only girl riding a motorcycle, and everybody knew me. Wherever I went, strangers said, "You're the one with the hot ride." I was hanging around with the boys, riding together and racing on the autobahn.

Mama didn't like it from the beginning and said, "I have never seen a girl on a motorcycle, this is a boy thing and it's too dangerous." The first time I wanted to give her a ride she said, "Only if you promise to go slow." If she liked to go to church or shopping she would ask me, "Gitta, can you give me a ride?" I knew she started to like it. All my friends liked to go for rides too and I would take them for a spin.

Home Sweet Home

I worked hard, sometimes with a lot of overtime, and saved my money. I promised myself I would take care of Mama.

"From now on, I want you to take it easy," I told her.

But she was not the kind of person to sit still and do nothing. "I have to keep busy."

There was a small place for sale, they were old barracks used by the military during the war. It had a large garden around it. Just being curious, I went to see it. The price was not too high, and I thought, this would be the perfect place for the two of us. The nice garden was something we both would have liked. Without telling Mama, I saved every penny and made a down payment.

One day Mama asked me, "Why aren't you're riding the motorcycle so often, or going out with your friends?" I came up with all kind of excuses. The day finally came and I paid off the rest of the house. I got the key, we shook hands and the deal was done. I was all excited to show Mama the new place, but was waiting for the right time.

The coming Sunday she asked, "Gitta, can you take me to church today?"

"Sure Mama, I'll be ready in a minute."

Of course I didn't drive to church, so Mama shouted at me, "This isn't the way to church."

"I know Mama, there is something I would like to show you."

When we arrived at the place she asked, "Why are you bringing me here?" and next she yelled, "Oh look at this nice big garden."

That's what I wanted to hear from her, I knew that she liked it. "Come on Mama, I'd like to show you the inside of the house."

As I opened the door she was more confused and said, "How can you go into other peoples houses, don't people live here?"

"It's not other people's, it's ours Mama!"

"What do you mean ours, how can this be ours?" She looked at me with her eyes and mouth wide open and said, "Gitta, you didn't."

"Yes Mama, I did." She was overwhelmed, crying and running all over the place. It had a living room, two bedrooms, kitchen, bathroom and an outside shed.

"You like it Mama?"

"Of course I like it, it's wonderful, and you mean I can live here?"

"Yes, Mama this is our new sweet home, I want you to be happy and enjoy it." From all the excitement, she had forgotten about church. We moved out of the village, leaving all the pain and nightmares behind. I painted the inside and out, put up wallpaper and together we fixed up the garden. We planted roses, flowers and grew vegetables. There also were fruit trees and bushes with all kinds of berries. Mama enjoyed it very much and I never saw her so happy. I was working all day, and when I came home dinner was ready. We sat together and ate in peace. I didn't want any more memories of our life in Hell and I asked the farmer to take all of our old things to the dump. We thanked him for being so kind and helpful, and said we would stay in touch.

Mama had saved some money and said, "Gitta, the house is so empty, let's go shopping." We got new furniture and other things we needed. Finally, we lived in peace and enjoyed our cozy home. Mama said, "You see Gitta, *after all the rain, the sun is shining again.*"

"That wasn't rain Mama, it was a hurricane." But soon the blue skies would be covered with dark clouds again.

One thing that always concerned me was Mama's health. She went to the doctors often and took more and more medication for her heart condition. I knew she was in pain, but she never complained. With all the fruits and berries in our garden, Mama was the expert and she knew what to do with them.

Besides making jellies and marmalade, she had a recipe for making wine. It wasn't written down anywhere, only in her head. The preparation was very messy but when it came time to fill the bottles, it was the best tasting wine I ever had. Now we had more people visiting us. Before, everyone had been afraid or scared of Karl. Every time we had guests Mama liked to treat them with coffee, cake or a homemade glass of wine. All the guests would pay her compliments. Sometimes the farmer couple would come by with Peter. He was not the brightest one and lived with his parents at the farm.

"How is Lotti? I miss her very much," I asked.

"She had a baby boy, he looked just like her. Why don't you and your Mama come and visit us?"

"I would like to," I said, but it's not a good idea. It would bring back all the bad memories and this wouldn't be good for either of us, going back to the place in hell."

"We understand how you must feel," they said. Peter and I had lots of catching up to do. We still talked about the drunken chickens, but this time it was funny and his father said, "I will never forget that day," and we all laughed.

It was time for them to leave and on the way out Mama said, "It's nice to see you all, why don't you come back and visit?"

"We'll come back. We like your place, it's so warm and cozy."

CHAPTER VI

Life Behind the Iron Curtain

I mentioned before that we lived in the eastern part of Germany, controlled by the Russian Government. This was not the nicest place on earth to be. The country was isolated from the western world. Going on vacation was allowed only in other communist countries such as Russia, Poland, Romania and Czechoslovakia. It was a life behind the "Iron Curtain." There were shortages of almost everything. Bananas and oranges we saw only once a year, around Christmas time. The lines outside the store were so long you would wait for hours. If you were lucky you would get two or three pieces each, and not the best quality.

Most fruit came from Cuba, also a communist country. Sometimes when it was my turn, and someone behind the counter said, "Sorry we are all out." After standing for so long, going home—empty handed was very frustrating. We had the same problems with meat or other simple things like onions. This was a part of everyday life, standing in line and waiting. For most working people like me, there was a slim chance of getting anything. The stores closed at 6pm and were closed Saturday and Sundays. The ones who stayed home were the lucky ones. If we wanted a TV set you had to write your name in a book and wait. With only the East German and Russian Channels to watch in black and white, the government made sure through censorship that the people couldn't see what was happening in the western world. People became tired of this TV programming, and the TV business declined. It was forbidden by the government to listen to western music or watch western TV. But what about all of the propaganda they forced on us, telling us we lived in a free country? What a joke it was, the people weren't stupid. They knew it was propaganda.

If you wanted some luxury items like a refrigerator or washing machine, it was no problem. Just put your name on the list and wait. The longest waiting time was for a car, ten to fifteen years, and there were only four models available: A Russian Volga, an East German Trabant, an East German Wartburg and a Czechoslovakian Skoda. When your time came to pickup your car, you had no choice of color, you had to take it or leave it. People used to make fun and say, "All the old people are driving new cars." Having a connection was very helpful, paying under the table to avoid having to wait a long time for goods.

I had a radio at my workstation, and listened to English, American and West German music. Every time my boss, Kurt, walked by he would turn off my radio and I would turn it back on. He was very loyal to the communist party and brainwashed. This made him very dangerous; he could report you and destroy your life. Because of that he was not well liked. Somebody told me that he joined the Nazi Party, and now he belonged to the communist party. He had switched from brown to red.

One day Bill my coworker came to work wearing a new pair of jeans, which he got from his uncle in America. Kurt told him to go home and change his pants. They had a big argument. Bill had a western attitude and returned the very next day wearing his new jeans just to make the boss's day. I liked Bill; his attitude was a lot like mine. When he arrived the next day, he came over to me and we gave each other a high five. Kurt was such a fanatic it was sickening. If he saw someone smoke a cigarette that was not made in a communist country he would take it away and step on it.

There was always a feeling of being watched, and the people were bitter and very unhappy. The situation was so bad that people didn't trust each other anymore. Even the children in kindergarten and schools were brainwashed. If their parents said anything against the government, the children would report their parents to the teacher and soon after their parents would be questioned and put in jail. On Election Day they made sure everyone voted for the Communist Party. I remember it was on a Sunday before noon, two men knocked on my door and asked me, "Why aren't you voting? It's your duty as a citizen."

"I am not going" I answered. They got angry and left, and one came back in the afternoon. He started to argue with me and began to yell and push me around. That made me angry so I kicked him out the door. The next morning at work my boss said, "I heard you didn't vote yesterday and what happened at your house." I was prepared for his questioning and I gave him the right answer, "The government tells me that I live in a free country and nobody can make me do something against my will." It was the truth; he was speechless and walked away. The government told the people how lucky they were to live in this part of the world, because the western society was poisonous.

What was wrong with this picture? People knew what was going on, but they kept quiet and were afraid to speak up. We couldn't use our own brain to think, the government did it for us. There were so many things we had to do, and could not do, it was just too much, like being tied to a leash. The whole situation was so tense that a bomb could go off at any time, because the people were very angry and unhappy.

In order to get western currency, the government opened stores called Inter Shop. This was not meant to benefit the East German people; it was for the visitors from the western world. It was designed to give the appearance that East Germany had the same quality of life as the western world. It was an allusion. Once in a while I went with friends to check it out. Being curious, we could not buy anything because we didn't' have the required foreign money. It was painful to see all these nice things that we couldn't have.

Every time I went on vacation in other Communist countries, people always asked for deutsche marks, or dollars. When I would tell them that I was from East Germany, they would walk away; my money was worthless. This could be very frustrating and make you feel like a black sheep. If I wanted to go to a concert or other event, I was always told, "Sorry we can't accept your money." The only way was to exchange the Eastern Mark into the local currency, but it cost and arm and a leg to do so, and it made your vacation not as enjoyable.

After waiting two years, the day came for me to pick up a TV set. People who had one would turn their roof antennas in the direction of the East German approved TV stations, but mine went the other way. I was able to watch the West German channels and American Movies. They came on after midnight and I didn't miss one of them. One day a man came and told me in a mean voice, "You have to move the antenna in the other direction."

I answered, "I don't think so, that's the way I like it. If you have any problems with this, fix it yourself." Sure enough, he climbed up the ladder to the roof and turned the big antenna around. He thought he solved the problem but he didn't know me. After he left, I climbed up and turned the antenna my way. One week later he came back, and argued with me and left very angry. I never saw him again. I think he finally gave up on me knowing I was so stubborn.

When Germany was divided, so were many families. The ones who lived in the West were the lucky ones. They were allowed to visit the East by car or by a special train from the Bundesbahn. To see them with nice cars and clothes was very upsetting. I asked myself, why don't we have all of these nice things, we are Germans too? The two Germanys became two different worlds like day and night. There was no choice of escaping, you would risk your life and get killed trying to cross the border. Many times I asked myself, "If we all just stick together it would make a difference, and we could get out of this miserable life of ours." But me, I was always an outsider. If somebody said yes, I would say no, and I would try to solve problems my way, not all of course, but some.

When I was twenty years old I had to face a very painful experience. After many years of suffering from the flue and colds, because of the cold and wet months, I developed a very bad sinus infection. I suffered from extreme headaches. It came to a point where I couldn't take it anymore and went to see a doctor. He was an ear, throat and nose specialist and the only one in the city. His private practice was in his own private villa. After he made x-rays he said, "Oh my god, this looks very bad. You need surgery!"

He made me return the next morning for preparations. The only thing I knew was that the area would be sensitive and painful. After they gave me a shot to calm me down, I was taken into the surgery. Before I lay down on the table, I couldn't believe my eyes. There was a dog with long ears, an English Hound that belonged to the doctor. What in the world was this dog doing in the operating room? It was unbelievable! My arms and legs were tied down with big leather belts and at that moment I knew that this was going to be bad. A nurse numbed my forehead with ice, and then I saw the doctor with an electric drill in his hand, which freaked me out. He is not going to use this on me, I thought. Two nurses held my hand and I heard the Doctor saying, "This is going to hurt." The next moment I heard the sound from the drill, and I felt pressure on my head. I heard myself screaming as the drill went deeper and deeper into my skull. The pain I felt was so severe I almost blacked out. Blood was running down my face and into my eyes.

"Okay," the doctor said, "this one is done, I have to do this one more time." If I weren't tied down to the table I would have jumped and run. My whole body was shaking, scared of the pain that I had just experienced. He started again and halfway down, the drill broke, and a piece half a finger long was stuck in my head. I heard him say, "*Scheisse*," as he tried to get it out. I felt like I was losing my mind. The two nurses had a hard time holding my head still. The pain was indescribable; it was the worst I ever felt. Finally, he removed the broken piece and finished the drilling. This was torture to me, but the only words he said to me were, "You are a very brave patient."

I was so exhausted from fighting the pain I was unable to speak. After I got cleaned up, I had two metal drain tubes sticking out of my forehead, right between my eyes. My head was bandaged. Every morning the doctor had a large needle with liquid that he injected into the drain holes. I was sitting in a chair holding a plastic container in front of me and I saw all the infected fluids drain out of my nose. It was disgusting to see. He did this procedure for about seven days until fluid began to be clear. We underestimate our body because it's amazing how much pain we can take. I just wondered if there was another way to take care of this problem without torturing someone like that. To this day I still have the scars. It was on March 10th, 1960, and yet another unpleasant time in my life to remember

I started to go out dancing and partying with my friends. To dance was not a problem, but dating was a different story. In every guy I saw my Grandpa's face, and in my mind they were all just like him. But after some time I realized that not everyone was like that. A friend of mine invited my girlfriend and me to a New Year's party. There was a very handsome guy looking at me. We danced and spent the whole time together, and during the early morning hours he asked me if he could walk me home. His name was Thomas, and as he left he said, "I would like to see you again." I liked him and thought he was very polite and I said yes. Every free moment we had we spent together. We went to movies, rode bikes, hiked and played all kinds of sports. In the winter we went skiing and ice-skating. Whatever we did was fun and we enjoyed each other's company.

On some weekends we went for a picnic by a lake, river or in the mountains. He was outgoing just like me. After some time he introduced me to his mom, but I had the feeling that she was not happy to meet me. For me it was the first time I had met a boyfriend's Mom. I wasn't too concerned about it because I just wanted to be with him. Every time he took me to his home she was not very nice to me.

The next summer on my twenty-first birthday, Thomas asked me, "Gitta, have you ever been to Berlin?"

"No."

"Neither have I. What do you think about us going to the big city on vacation?"

I liked that idea and was very excited.

His mother was upset, but my Mama said, "That's wonderful, you two will have a good time, just be careful."

Chapter VII

Brandenburger Gate of The Berlin Wall 1961

W e started to make plans for our big trip. Thomas had just finished serving the required two and a half years in the Air Force in order to become a college engineering student in the fall. I signed up for a vacation and we studied the map, packed our belongings on my BMW motorad and off we went on the autobahn. After a long ride we arrived late at night in Berlin. We set up the tent on a lake outside the city called Mueggelsee. First thing in the morning we went to see the big city. To get there we had to take a boat across the lake. This was my first time in a big city away from home. It was very exciting for us. There was so much to see and so many places to go. The traffic, all the people running around like ants and all the nice stores and restaurants were great. We shopped in Berlin's most famous street, Die Kurfuerstendam. We rode on the U Bahn and the S Bahn, and saw the movie "Bridge on the River Kwai," with William Holden. We whistled the marching song from the movie all the time. We sang Elvis songs at the open fire on the lake; he was our favorite. We also saw Bill Haley in concert. We learned how to sing in English without understanding the lyrics. We had a wonderful time together and got a taste of big city life.

Suddenly, after one week, things began to change. Everywhere we went there were officials in uniforms, and we were asked for our ID's. We had to show it everywhere we went. There were checkpoints on every corner and signs saying, "You are leaving the Soviet Zone and are entering the American, British or French Zones." We had no idea what this was all about. It was very disturbing and confusing. At one checkpoint, we were delayed for several hours in the burning heat and our ID's were taken away. They even called the police station in our hometown and asked if we had a political background.

I said to Thomas, "I don't like this. Something fishy is going on, what could it be?" But no matter how many questions we asked there were no answers. Our vacation came to an end and so did our money. It was hard for us to leave after all the fun we had enjoyed. On the way to the autobahn, we were stopped at several checkpoints and asked why we came to Berlin. We were searched everywhere, so was the motorcycle. They took some clothes and magazines away, being very rude and treating us like criminals. It was all very confusing for Thomas and me, and we didn't have a good feeling about all this. Something was going on, but we couldn't solve the puzzle, there were too many pieces missing. We left the city on August 12th, drove all night and arrived the next morning at home.

Mama was waiting for us, crying and upset. "Oh my God, oh my God, I am so glad to see you back. You won't believe what happened over night. These damn Communists split Berlin and built a wall dividing it." Mama was upset; this was the first time I ever heard her swear.

"Mama, "calm down, this must be a mistake."

"No, no, I heard it on the radio."

"This is not possible Mama, we just came from there." While we were driving home on the autobahn that night, the wall was being built. We were in shock, but now we had answers to all of the strange happenings we experienced in Berlin, the missing puzzle pieces now fit. That was August 13th 1961; I was twenty-one years old. It shocked the whole world and was written in the history books. I was there in the last free hours of this beautiful city. This was the end of freedom for millions of Germans. They would live behind the Iron Curtain for many years to come.

It was my first vacation and I would never forget it, it was a happy one but also a tragic one. People panicked and were in shock and disbelief. Many tried to escape in different ways; some tried to swim channels or rivers, thru underground tunnels, by small planes, cars, trucks and even hot air balloons. There were a few lucky ones, but most were either shot or blown up by land mines. A friend of mine escaped on a stormy and rainy night by crawling on her stomach thru a muddy potato field. She was lucky and made it to the west.

Breaking Up Is Hard To Do

Thomas and I were still together, but after we came back from vacation trouble in paradise started. He went back to school and we didn't see each other that often, only on some weekends. Whenever he asked me to come to his house his mom was even worse and barely talked to me. Every time Thomas said we liked to do something together, she would keep him busy all day and night. She got mad if he put his arm around me or gave me a kiss and never had anything nice to say about me. She said things like "Thomas, why do you have to hang on her all the time?"

I took her flowers, pralines and helped clean the house and garden, but nothing I did was appreciated. One day I asked Thomas, "I have the feeling that your Mom does not like me."

"That's not true, just give her more time," he said.

I waited and waited but the situation just got worse. Sometimes we went out with friends and if it was late he asked me to stay overnight, and I would sleep on the couch. She wouldn't go to bed, leaving her door open, sneaking back and forth watching us. Then she would demand Thomas to get her a pill, make tea and say things like "it's late, come to bed." She kept him busy so we couldn't be alone together. This happened every time I stayed there and it was very upsetting to me. I told my girlfriend what was bothering me and she said, "Gitta, what's the matter with you? Are you blind, don't you see what she is up to? She's jealous of you."

"How can she be jealous of me?" People say that love is blind, maybe it's true. I was confused, and I didn't know what to think about what was going on behind their closed doors. He was twenty-three years old and sleeping in the same bed with his Mom. I wondered, should I tell Mama? I decided not to, I didn't want to bother her with my problems, because she and Thomas liked each other very much and he always treated her with respect. If I got flowers Mama got some, if I got a present Mama also got something. He was always polite and a gentleman. So I didn't say anything to Mama; maybe it was entirely my fault? On Christmas Eve Mama asked him if he wanted to come to our house.

"I would like that very much," and he came in the afternoon. We exchanged presents, sat around the tree, sang songs, had a nice dinner and a very delightful evening. That night there was a big snowstorm, so Mama asked Thomas to stay the night. The next morning the storm cleared and we went to his Moms' house to give her presents and wish her a Merry Christmas. I had a bad feeling, and Thomas looked very nervous and didn't say much. We arrived, saying Merry Christmas, but she didn't answer, and her face hung towards the ground.

She started to yell, looking at her son, "Where have you been all night, did you have fun with this whore?" I couldn't believe that she called me this name and how much she hurt my feelings, because I was always faithful to her son. I cried and ran back home.

Thomas came after me, "Gitta, please don't go, I love you!"

I turned to him and said, "Leave me alone and go back to your Mom."

Mama was surprised to see me back so soon and asked, "What happened and why are you crying?" After I calmed down she shook her head and said, "A lady doesn't talk like that. That was a horrible thing to say and that was not very nice. And what did Thomas say?"

"Nothing Mama, he just stood there."

"It's better if you don't go there anymore." I took Mama's advice. Thomas was embarrassed and apologized.

"What's wrong with your Mom and what's wrong with you? Why is she so mean to me and why didn't you say anything?" He was silent and just walked away. "What a wimp", I thought; he didn't even try to protect me. Now I had mixed feelings, this would not work out in the long run. There would not be a happy ending for us. I tried to understand and make excuses for his mom's behavior. Her husband had passed away one year earlier, was that the reason? But she wasn't alone, her daughter, son-in-law and two grandsons lived next door to her. Was she afraid to lose her only son? I was twenty-three years old, had a good job, owned a small house and had a motorcycle. Thomas was in college and had nothing. Every time we went out I was embarrassed because he barely had any clothes to wear. I bought him a nice suit, shoes, shirt and sweater, even a winter coat.

But all his mom said was, "Thomas, you must be doing something good to her, she keeps buying you all this stuff." She never bought him anything, why couldn't she say something nice? What was wrong with her? What was it, why didn't she like me? I couldn't figure it out. We still saw each other but not often. I felt the damage inside me but still loved him.

On New Years Eve he said, "Gitta, I love you and would like to marry you."

"I don't know Thomas, what about your mom, she won't like this."

"It's going to be okay, don't worry. Why don't you come with me and I will tell her?"

I was very worried; this could be a disaster. If I were to go it would only be because of him. I hadn't seen her for a while and tried to be nice. After Thomas told her of our plan she started to scream hysterically. "I will never give my permission, never, never, only over my dead body. And what about me?"

All Thomas said was, "But mom," but she kept yelling.

For me this was a wakeup call and it opened my eyes. I grew brave, went to her and said, "I don't know what kind of a mother you are, but you can have him all for yourself. You don't have to worry about me anymore. Don't forget to lock him up in the glass cabinet, just to look at and not touch! And one more thing, I feel sorry for the next girl he will bring home one day!"

I was angry but felt some relief and left. I knew something would happen, I just knew.

Thomas came to me and said, "Please Gitta, don't go away so angry."

"Thomas, enough is enough, your mom's behavior is not normal, and you are not man enough to speak up. I'm sorry but it's better if we don't see each other anymore. As long as your Mom is around we will never be happy."

"But I love you Gitta."

"I love you too Thomas."

From the beginning we had a strong relationship but in the end it was destroyed. By whom I am not sure, maybe we all played a part, not taking the time to communicate and understand each other. Would it have made any difference? I don't know.

My heart was broken and after over four years of being together, I said goodbye. We both had tears in our eyes.

Mama was very sad. "I am sorry for you Gitta, It was not meant to be. Whatever happens in life there is a reason for it."

I tried to keep busy and forget but it wasn't easy. I remembered the conversation I had earlier with my girlfriend. How come it took me so long to realize, but what people say is probably true, "Love can make you blind, and has the power to make you float in the clouds."

One month later Thomas came to apologize and asked for a second chance, but I told him, "No." I wasn't sure if I made the right decision, but at that time it felt right. One thing I knew for sure is that we loved each other, maybe because he was my first boyfriend and I was his first girlfriend. The power of love pushed my feelings away. This was the end of my first love and to this day I think of him.

As a mother you always wish the best for your child. That day I made a promise to myself, if I were to ever have a child and the time came for them to start dating, I would never stand between them. I wanted to be caring, loving and understanding. This promise I would always keep. Now I spent more time with Mama and my friends. After some time went by I started dating again, but nothing serious. I would always think about Thomas.

I worried about Mama; she was not going in the garden so often anymore. She enjoyed it very much but now she spent most of her time in the house or in bed. She never complained but I knew she was in pain. I made sure she took her medication, prepared meals and was around her as much a possible.

One day she was lying down and called me into her bedroom. "Gitta, please come to me and listen to my heart." Seeing her face and holding her chest I knew she was in pain and very ill. I laid my head on her chest and it sounded like a waterfall. I knew this was serious, and took her to Dr. Amarell immediately.

After he examined her he said to me, "Gitta your Mama has to go to the hospital. She's very sick, it's her heart." I was scared and remembered what Mama told me a long time ago, "If I ever have to go to the hospital, I will never come out alive." Every day I went to see her, in the morning on my way to work and at lunchtime in the afternoon. Whenever I saw her, her condition grew worse. After she was in the hospital for two weeks, something strange happened in our house. Mamas' bedroom was next to mine, and one night at exactly twelve o'clock I heard her calling my name. It's not possible I thought, she's is in the hospital. I must be having a bad dream."

The next morning I went to see her but her bed was empty. My heart started to race, I ran to the nurse and asked where Mama was. She showed me a room down the hall where I saw Mama all by herself. I cried when I saw the condition she was in. Her feet were very swollen; the look in her blue eyes was so distant.

"Water," she whispered, "please give me water."

I gave her a drink, and laid my body over hers and cried like I never had before. It was so painful to see her suffer and not be able to help. I was not sure if she still recognized me.

"Mama it's me, your Gitta, I will be back at noon."

On my way out she said very quietly, "I am not here at noon, I love you goodbye!" These were the last words I heard from her. At noon that day she left me forever, it was on December 28th 1966 shortly after her 66th birthday. I was twenty-six, my world had stopped but the rest of the world kept going.

In Pain and All Alone

The darkest days of my life had knocked on the door. I was always afraid for this day to come but not so soon. My heart was broken and it was hard for me to let go. It felt like somebody ripped my heart out. The pain I felt was indescribable, my body was numb and I felt empty inside. I had lost the person I loved the most. She did so much for me, living only for me. She had been the only caring and loving person in my life. Mama was never angry, even if I deserved it. I had to admit that I was not perfect, nobody is, but when I was at a certain age, I thought I knew everything about life. I didn't want to take advice, and even talked back without knowing how I hurt Mamas feelings. I felt badly after having said the words, but my excuse was that this was part of growing up.

When things went wrong, Mama was right, and I wished I had listened to her. I took her in my arms, apologized and said, "I am so sorry Mama, and I didn't mean to hurt you."

"It's okay Gitta, I can't be mad at you because you are all I have. You are my life."

These words changed my attitude and I was never disrespectful again. I wished I never behaved as I did, and wished I could take it back. How could I be so rude, dumb, and stupid? She taught me to be polite, honest and to respect other people. So many times she told me how much she loved me, how could she leave me? Mama was a one of a kind, a wonderful human being and I would never meet someone like her again.

Now I was all alone with no family. I was hurt, angry at the whole world, and everything around me. At the funeral I fell apart, became hysterical and went to the hospital with a nervous breakdown. I didn't want to live anymore and was on suicide watch. All I wanted was to be next to my Mama.

After three weeks I was released, but whatever I did, or where ever I went, Mama was always on my mind. All of a sudden, my life was empty and senseless. As we all know, time heals all wounds but my pain never went away. The two of us had gone through so much together. I never before felt the pain of losing someone I loved so much. I knew Mama was not suffering anymore and was watching me from above, to make sure her little girl was ok. Why didn't I tell her more often how much I loved her, why didn't I say, "Thank you. Why, why, why? I love you my guardian angel, thinking about you all the time and miss you very much. Without you I would not be the person I am, because you did a wonderful job raising me. Thank you for everything my love, thank you for being my Mama!"

Things changed for me after Mama passed away because nothing was the same anymore. The Christmas times we spent together, which used to be my favorite time of the year was silently swept away. I was very lonesome with no family and afraid to face the reality. For years I locked myself up and cry all though the night; the same on New Year's Eve. At midnight I would listen to the radio and hear the bells ringing from all over the world and how people celebrate the New Year, but I was sad, depressed and would cry. I was in that state until my son, Michael, was born.

Then the lights on the Christmas tree started shining again and he became the bright, glimmering star. This little, sweet and innocent boy was the best medicine and helped me get over my depression. I regained my confidence again; it's amazing how powerful a child can be. He took my pain away and brought inspiration back into my life. I thank him for that and love him even more. I am very fortunate to have him who I call "my son."

After so many cloudy and rainy days I saw the sunshine again.

Embarrassing Moments

Going on vacation in other communist block countries could be a very unpleasant experience and we were only allowed to travel in groups. There were always two or three "brain-washed people" present to keep an eye on the group. We used to call them "Red Bulls," a reference to the communist party. There was a big difference in the way you were treated depending if you came from the West or the East. For example, we stayed in a Hungarian hotel in Budapest. The big dining room was divided with a wall; one side was for the tourists from the West and the other from the East. We were told not to cross over to the western area. I was curious to find out what was on the other side of the wall. After I used the bathroom, I walked to the other side. What a difference! There was wine on the table, flowers, lobster, steak and even caviar. As I made my way back to our area, one of the Red Bulls came looking for me. He was not very nice; he asked me what I was doing over there.

"I got lost," I answered. It was too late; I saw what I wanted to see. We had water and chicken, and I was thinking to myself, politics and money talk. This situation continued in every country we visited. It was embarrassing and made us feel rejected.

During the summer of July 1968 one of my vacation trips was to Russia. The package included six days in Moscow and six days on the Black Sea. Just when I thought I had seen it all, in the other communist countries including East Germany, there was no comparison with the way the Russians celebrated the power of communism. What a sight, everything was massive and on a huge scale. There were statues of Stalin, Lenin and other Communist leaders. One day we stood in long lines in front of the Saint Basilius Cathedral at Red Square with many other tourists. To the left across the street was a big building with the letters GUM. We were told that it was a shopping mall that used to be a female prison. The plan was to check it out after our tour. After the tour was over we met some German-speaking tourists from Austria. One of the red bulls came and said, "You're not allowed to speak to those people." I never forgot how upset they were and how embarrassing it was for us. What were they so afraid of, that we would find out how much better life was in the free world? The East German Government told the people that they had to build the wall to protect us from the Western enemy. What nonsense that was, there was no enemy.

We went inside the mall that used to be a prison. Nothing had changed and it was clear that it use to be a prison even with all the vendors there. It was hot, smelly and noisy. It was on our last day in Moscow and we were flying to the Black Sea the next day. The Red Bulls said, "Today you are on your own." I was very surprised because they had never left our side. Maybe they were up to something?

The five of us girls went for one last walk through the city. It was hot and muggy and we tried to find something cold to drink. We saw what looked like a restaurant and went inside. The first thing I noticed was that there were all men sitting down. They all turned around at the same time, staring at us like we had come from another planet. The waiter was running from one table to another and ignored us. When we asked for a cold drink he refused and told us to leave, this bar was for men only. I never had heard of such a thing in my life and didn't know what to think about all of this. We left without arguing and feeling embarrassed. We were guests in that country and had to be polite and respectful. From my own experience I learned that in different countries strange things could happen.

As a tourist the buses would take you to all the nice places. Our tour guide was a very nice lady who spoke German. We had a conversation about our life styles. She was surprised at how we lived and how much money we earned, which did not seem like much for us. My husband is a doctor, she said, he is driving with a motorcycle in poor condition to see patients. He makes less money than you people. We knew most of the Russian people were poor but a doctor? It was unbelievable.

When we walked around the city some individuals showed us big bundles of rubles and wanted to buy our clothes. In the hotel it was the same. The cleaning girls asked us for lingerie and clothes. Some of us tried to separate from the group to explore places where tourists were not allowed. A ride in a taxi was surprisingly cheap, and we saw many things we were not supposed to see. Something caught my eye; all the windows were covered with newspapers instead of curtains.

Another embarrassing moment occurred when we went to the Black Sea, near the Turkish border. It was a beautiful place with all the tropical plants and palm trees. The beach had no sand and was covered with black stones. Walking around without sandals was impossible because of the hot, black rocks. The climate was subtropical, and it was hot and muggy so we couldn't go outside for several hours during the day in order to avoid the heat. The rooms had no air conditioning or fans and it was not very comfortable. We weren't used to these conditions, and some of us would faint, others get diarrhea. The food was so different that it also gave us problems. One girl became so sick that she had to be hospitalized and on our final day she had to stay behind. There weren't too many people out during the daytime, but during the night, everyone came out, even the locals with their babies. But to our surprise, after eleven o'clock at night, no one was allowed to be on the streets. The police walked around, blowing whistles rounding up stragglers. They had some strange and different laws.

There was a bazaar in town and we went to check it out. The tropical fruits interested us the most, because we didn't have them at home. As we walked around an elderly woman suddenly attacked us. She started to beat us with a stick. We didn't know what this was all about and we ran for cover. Some people tried to hold her back and calm her down. Shortly we found out why she became so wild. We were speaking German and it triggered her crazy behavior. We were told that she had lost her husband in the war. This incident was very embarrassing for us in front of so many people. In all the years after the war, Germany had a bad reputation and the entire world pointed a finger at us. In some countries people called me Nazi, Hitler girl and even spit in my face. I never hurt anyone in my life and was an innocent victim like millions of others. This prejudice would hurt my feelings and make me very sad. However I tried not to let it ruin my vacation.

A friend of mine met a couple at the beach that invited us to their place. We couldn't believe what we saw. They lived in one room, sharing it with a donkey, goat and some chickens. It was messy, smelly, hot and had no running water, air-conditioning or toilet. I saw mothers breast-feeding their babies in public. That was not a big deal to them, unlike in East Germany. Women at the beach lay in their underpants and bras and it seemed like they didn't care. This was another world with a different culture. My friend could not get over what we saw and kept saying, "Look over there or look at that one."

"Be quiet, just pretend like we didn't see it. If you don't stop staring, they might notice and come after us."

Chapter VIII

The Old City

Time passed slowly after Mama passed away. I decided to sell my little home and move to the city. I found a place in a historic house; on the second floor with two rooms and a small kitchen. But shortly afterwards I realized I had made a big mistake in selling the house and I was very angry with myself. The thing I missed most about it was the big garden. After all that had happened I tried to focus on the positive side. Everything was more convenient, my job was closer, and the hospital across the street and stores were all within walking distance. I said to myself, you can't have everything perfect, just get used to it."

The city was very old and unique. It was 1300 years old. It had many churches, castles and other historic buildings. The homes were built out of clay, wood or bricks and were connected by narrow, cobblestone streets. One famous composer lived there from 1703-1707; his name was Johann Sebastian Bach. He was an organist in a big church that was named after him. Our blind friend used to play on the same organ. Many generations of this musical family used to live in this city. There were rumors that Bach got himself in big trouble, because of his numerous affairs with women. The Mayor suspended him from entering the city, but later called him back to play the organ once again. If that was true or not I did not know, but that was the local story.

A special attraction was the Baroque Dolls Town "Mon Plaisir" in the palace museum, with about 82 houses and 400 dolls. It is the largest collection of historic dollhouses in the world. The city was ideal for shooting movies. Years later my son and I were extras in a movie called "The Little Mozart." The city shared the title of Oldest City in Germany with another city called Trier. In 1581 the Old City had a serious fire that destroyed 378 houses, the town hall, renaissance church and other attractive buildings. When a city is that old it has many stories to tell. From the rich to the poor, from illnesses like Typhus and Cholera, it was quite a story from the founding of the city to the 20th century.

After waiting for several years with my name on a list, I finally was approved to move into a new apartment. It was like taking steps backward in time. There were no elevators or no electric heaters. There was just a big ceramic oven that had to be heated with wood and charcoal. Getting the wood and coal was done using buckets; I would walk down to the basement, load the buckets and carry them up to the 5th floor. This was very difficult and labor intensive. The only nice thing about the apartment was the view. This is what the East German Government called modern and luxury living, and showed how well they really took care of their citizens. Whenever I think about living behind the Iron Curtain it turns my stomach and makes me sick. There is so much hatred and anger inside me against the communist regime.

To get over my painful loss, I was active in all kinds of sports and travel. But there was nothing that could heal me physically and mentally. I thought, "I can't go on like this, it's going to eat me up. How can I heal myself?" Being alone wasn't the answer. A baby, how about having a baby? It would change everything, getting me out of my depression and giving me a large responsibility. That's it, I want to have a baby and raise it just like Mama raised me, with lots of love! I think I would make a good mother and Mama would be proud of me.

One day I met a man who was good-looking and very charming. He took me to nice restaurants, brought flowers, presents and treated me like a lady. His name was Frank and after being with him for three years I became pregnant.

"Something is wrong with you," he said one day, "why don't you go and get a pregnancy test?"

I noticed that I felt differently and that I had morning sickness. The day I went to see the Doctor, it was raining very hard. After examining me he said that I was 3 months pregnant.

When I came home Frank was waiting for me and asked, "What did the Doctor say?"

"Not much, he gave me a piece of paper."

When he looked at it, he started yelling, "I knew it, I knew it!"

"If this is so, why are you so surprised and upset?" I asked.

For me it was good news but he said, "You're going to have an abortion, right?"

"You must be out of your mind saying such a thing," I said. "Of course I am having this baby, it's my baby and nothing can stop me!"

Becoming a father is easy, but being one is a different story. I knew he was a ladies' man and after he asked me to marry him I said no. Having a baby was fine with me. I wasn't showing much until the end of my pregnancy. I wore a coat or thick jacket because it was wintertime. Nobody noticed I was pregnant, only those I told. I prepared myself for that big day to come. I bought a book on how to change diapers, the details of giving birth and everything else a mother should know. I practiced changing diapers with a juice bottle, using the bottle as a baby. My suitcase was already packed and after my water broke I went to the hospital that was one block away. I knew that the delivery room was on the third floor. I arrived with a suitcase in my hand and a pillow under my arm. When I looked at my watch it showed eleven P.M.

A nurse came and asked, "What do you want? This is the delivery room."

"I know, does it look like I am going on vacation?"

She laughed and asked, "Are you having a baby?"

I took my coat off and said, "Look at me!"

"Oh, okay, come with me." It was a difficult birth after being in labor for over thirty hours.

I was screaming from the pain. The midwife, who was a fat lady, said, "You weren't crying before when you got pregnant."

That made me angry and I asked her, "Have you ever had a baby?"

"No" she said.

During the next contraction, she turned around and reached for something and said, "Push." At that moment I kicked her in the butt, she hit the floor and the baby arrived. My birth canal broke and needed stitches. I wanted a boy so badly, but first I asked, "Is the baby okay, is everything normal?"

The doctor said, "It's a boy, a healthy baby boy!"

This was January 13th, 1972 at 03:50 in the morning. I was holding my bundle of joy; it was the happiest moment of my life.

A Mother's Nightmare

I named my baby Michael. On his birth certificate I marked it father unknown. All my friends came with flowers and balloons to see us. Only Frank did not show up. Of course I was hurt, but I had other things to worry about. I noticed something was wrong. My baby was different from the others, he was much smaller, constantly crying and vomiting. I told the nurses and the doctors, but they just laughed and said, "You are not the youngest and this is your first baby. Nothing is wrong and you worry too much."

I was thirty-two years old at the time, but no matter what they said, my motherly instincts told me that my baby was very ill. We were released from the hospital; mother and baby were okay; at least that's what the papers said.

Normally the ambulance would take us home, but living as close as I did it wasn't necessary. My girlfriend helped me out, walked us home and even heated the house. I remember how cold it was that day, 22 degrees below zero. Two days later, Frank came with flowers and baby supplies. He bent over the crib and asked, "What is it? A boy or girl?"

"What do you care, you didn't come when I needed you."

"I'm sorry," he said, "A business trip was holding me up." He was good at making excuses and not being honest. How often he used to say, "Look at me, do you think these green eyes could lie? Let's get married and be a family."

"I don't think so. I'm going to raise this baby without you."

"It's my baby too," he said.

"I know it's your baby, and besides the business trips you have lied to me. I know better. You're seeing another woman, your friends talk." This was the end of our relationship.

My babies' condition got worse; he cried day and night and rejected his milk. A few days later, I went to a doctor and told her how worried I was. After she examined my baby she made a phone call and told me, "Your baby is very ill, you have to bring him to the hospital immediately."

I still remember the faces of the ones who told me my baby was okay. I blamed myself and wondered what I had done wrong. The next day I went back and what I saw was heartbreaking. This poor little child was only 2 weeks old and was hooked up to several IV's all over his body. It was frightening and it hurt so much seeing him in this condition, not knowing what was wrong. I asked the doctor, and he said he was not sure at this point, "We will have to run more tests."

I was scared of losing my baby. I felt so helpless. Every night, sometimes until after midnight, I stood in front of the hospital staring at my baby's window. All I saw were shadows going back and forth. Several days later the doctor said to me, "The results from the test show that your son has a hole in his stomach, and if he does not have surgery he will die of starvation. He will have to go to another hospital which specializes in babies, because our hospital does not perform this type of surgery."

I cried and asked, "Doctor, what did I do wrong?"

He replied, "Don't blame yourself, it's very rare for this to happen and it only affects boys."

Frank came the same day to see the baby, and after I told him my big problem he said, "I want to speak with the Doctor." Frank had taken some semesters at medical school and knew more than me and he had a long talk with the doctor confirming his diagnosis.

The doctor arranged the ambulance, notified the children's hospital and gave us the papers we needed. Two days later at 6 a.m. Frank and I drove in the ambulance with Michael for about six hours on the autobahn to reach the other city. It was very foggy that morning, I said to Frank, "I really appreciate your coming along."

"He's my son and I worry too."

I was sick, vomiting all over the ambulance, with Frank holding the baby for the entire journey. When we arrived we were told that the hospital was overcrowded. I saw beds in hallways with children in them. The doctor said we would have to put your baby in the hall until a bed is available. I didn't like it but what choice did I have? "Doctor, please, just help my baby and keep him alive."

I had made plans of how I would raise my baby, what a good mother I wanted to be. Now I wondered if it would ever happen. Why was I being punished, why? I was terrified; I couldn't stop crying, and did not want to lose my baby. This was my only chance at having a family again. This was a communist country; technology and medicine were very far behind the western world. In my son's case, the proper medicine wasn't available in any communist country. The Doctor asked me if I had any contacts in the west that could supply the needed medicine.

At that time I had no connections in the west. The doctors tried their best but my baby was fighting everyday for this life. I had to watch helplessly with a broken heart and I was a nervous wreck. I took all my vacation and some time off from my job and stayed in a nearby hotel to be close to my baby. One time when I visited I saw my son tied into a harness and hanging from a device, which was stretching his body. To see this as a mother was simply horrifying. The doctor said to me, "Your baby needs surgery to close the hole in his stomach, but he's too weak and won't survive. You will have to pray for a miracle." In addition to the available medication, he was fed around the clock thru an I.V.

After four months, the doctor came to me with a smile and said, "I have good news for you, your baby is improving. I think he is going to make it without surgery but he still has a long way towards recovery."

I was so happy that I kissed the doctor on the cheek. What a relief it was for me after so much worry and prayers. I thanked the doctors and nurses for everything they had done for us. To show my appreciation I gave them packs of very expensive and rare coffee. My son was transferred to another hospital in the same city. I had been riding a train for six hours one way three times a week to see him.

One doctor said to me, "If something happens we will send you a telegram because you don't have a phone." This was nerve racking for me; every time someone came to my door I thought it might be a telegram with bad news about Michael. But he got better, he started gaining weight and finally the day came when he was ready to go home even though he was still weak. The doctor said, "We did everything we could; now it's up to Mother Nature. Sometimes when the body grows it heals by itself, if not we can operate when he is older and stronger."

I couldn't wait to take him in my arms after such a long time. It was a very happy day! Frank came, which was very nice of him.

The doctor gave us instructions on giving medicine and feeding Michael. I made sure that he had a lot of chicken soup and he started to look better everyday. He got his color back; his cheeks became round and after some time his arms filled out. I was feeling better and was happy to see him recovering after fighting for his life for over eight months.

He celebrated his first birthday, the second, third, was eating everything and grew up to be a healthy beautiful boy. It was a miracle that he survived. I wished my Mama could see him, so cute with his curly brown hair. I knew that she would have loved him just as much as she loved me. I loved Michael more than everything else in the world; I gave him all my love the way my Mama gave love to me.

When I was thirty-four years old, I had to be hospitalized to remove my gallbladder. Two days after surgery I had to stand up in front of the bed. I took my first step towards the window to look outside. To my surprise, I saw Michael with my neighbor standing and waving, he was just two years old. He was saying something but I couldn't hear him. I was shaky and weak and went back to bed, feeling overwhelmed after seeing him. Shortly afterwards he was standing next to my bed, somehow my neighbor managed to bring him into the intensive care room. I was so happy at that moment I forgot the surgery, pain and the ninety-four gallstones that had been removed.

"Mama, Mama," he said. With sparkling eyes he put his curly head on my chest and didn't want to let go. That was a most precious moment. It was so powerful, the bond between mother and child.

Reunion After Thirty Years

I was writing letters to stay in contact with Anna, my mama's sister. She was now in her late seventies and had health problems.

"Why don't you come and visit?" she asked.

I thought about going back one day but had mixed feelings. I was afraid of facing the past. But one day I decided to go, I packed my suitcase and took Michael on a long train ride. I was planning to go back to the city where I was born so many years ago, where hell on earth had started for me. I wanted to surprise everyone after so many years. I was already thirty-six, and my son was four years old, the same age when this story started. When we arrived, I called a taxi to take us to the house that was very close to the sea, on a hill, which looked like new. It had a beautiful view overlooking the beach and the sea.

When I knocked on the door, I was very nervous. A lady with curly blond hair opened the door. This must be Lena, I thought, Anna's daughter. The last time I saw her she must have been sixteen or seventeen years old.

I still remembered some Polish and asked, "I'm looking for a lady named Anna, and does she live here?"

She seemed to be confused but said, "Yes, she is my Mama. Mama, Mama, someone is here to see you." Shortly after, an old lady with white hair came around the corner and my heart almost stopped.

It was like my Mama was standing in front of me. She had the same gestures as Mama and me. I could feel my heart bounce against my throat and with a shaky voice I asked, "Do you remember me, I'm Gittchen?"

Her face suddenly changed, with her mouth and eyes wide open she started yelling, "Oh my god, oh my god, Gittchen is that you? What a surprise to see you, the last time I saw you, you were a little girl, and now you are a grown up woman standing in front of me!" We fell into each other's arms, overwhelmed with emotion, and we cried.

"Yes Aunt Anna, it's been a long time since we have seen each other." I introduced Michael to her and she welcomed us inside just like she did almost 30 years ago. The whole family came to see us: kids, grandkids, and great grandkids. We had many things to say and we talked about Mama

After a few days Aunt Anna asked me, "Would you like to see the city? I know you have bad memories, but nothing here will remind you of those days anymore." Lena and her husband Wadec were our tour guides and showed us around. I still remembered some places that had been destroyed and a shower of goose bumps came over me. In the next few minutes I flashed back; heard airplanes, people screaming and saw burning ruins; it was all in my head. A soft touch on my shoulder woke me from my memories; it was Lena asking if I was okay. I was fighting my emotions and began to cry.

We went to the elegant Grand Hotel where Mama had a job when she was young. We had a nice dinner and gambled in the casino. I wished Mama was with us, and for a moment I talked to her and asked if she could see me where I was. We went for a walk on the white sandy beach, the promenade, and wherever we went, it seemed as though nothing had ever happened here. These dark memories from my childhood remained. Now, people were laughing, having a good time, and enjoying life in this beautiful city. They sat in the beautiful cafes and restaurants or walked along the beach. It was just like Mama told me, how it used to be a long time ago.

A new generation was living here now, having learned about the past from history books or their parents and grandparents stories. Anna's family had planned a trip to visit the site of the Auschwitz Concentration camp. I wasn't looking forward to it. I had already visited Buchenwald, outside the city of Weimar, and knew how horrible it would be. I learned that Nazi doctors had cut skin from their victims to make wallets, handbags and lamps. What a horrible experience it was to see the ovens where they were burned. I also saw the prison cells where they would be shot in the back of the head or poisoned by gas. Behind the barracks was a hill where the survivors would have to dig holes and move rocks until they collapsed.

Seeing all this really got to me and made me sick in my stomach. Now, years later we were in Auschwitz and I had to re-live it all over again. I couldn't control my emotions; I imagined people screaming and the smell of dead bodies. I became ill from it. When I saw the railroad tracks to the camp, I remembered my early days and thought how lucky my Mama and I were. The cattle car we rode on hadn't brought us to one of these killing factories.

This was the biggest crime in modern human history, it should never be forgotten and we all must make sure it will never happen again. How could such a horrible thing take place? Sadly, the most shocking thing is the fact that the whole world watched, but failed to stop it.

Back at home, Aunt Anna opened her albums and we looked at pictures of when Mama and I used to live at her farm

"These pictures say a thousand words," I said.

"Yes they do, they will be memories for the rest of our lives."

It was very touching for me, reliving so many moments from the past. "I remember the times living on your farm very clearly," I said.

"I am sure", she said. "This was a difficult time in your life which you will never forget. If you would like to have some pictures you are welcome to take them."

"I would like to, thank you very much. What happened to the farm?"

"After you and your Mama left, the government took our identity away from us, along with the farm, which was my life."

"I am sorry so many valuable things were taken away from you."

Sadly, she said, "yes, that's true, but they could not take my memories from me."

Everybody was very warm and friendly to us. To my surprise, they all spoke German, even the little ones. "You see Gittchen," Aunt Anna said, "we are Polish citizens now, but deep in our hearts we are still Germans." Our vacation came to an end and it was time to go home. It was nice to see Mamas' relatives and I knew she appreciated me being there. My mission had been accomplished. A big party was arranged for us and many people came. Every one was so nice they made us feel like we were part of this big family. My Mama had been one of these sweet and generous people. It was hard to say goodbye, it was a bittersweet moment because I knew we would never see each other again.

I will never forget these dark days. How they had destroyed my childhood and many years of my life. Do I regret going back? Honestly, no, because it was a healing therapy that allowed me to gain closure with my past and go on with the rest of my life.

CHAPTER IX

My Big Dream

Ever since I was a teenager, I had dreamed of living in America, the land of the free and endless opportunities; a place where people say, "If you dream, dream big." When Mama was still alive she got a letter from California from her daughter who was married to a German and lived in America. Mama and I looked at the map together and I remembered her saying, "America, California, oh my god, that's so far away over the big ocean." For the first time I wrote a letter to my birth mom telling her the sad new about Mama's death. She wrote back to me and expressed how sorry she was. I was always thinking about how I could escape this miserable life of the communist regime. There was no future for Michael, so I wanted to give him a better life in a free society.

Sometimes things happen, and when they do they often work out in your favor. One day I received a letter from my birth mothers' husband, asking if I would like to come to America. At that time they didn't know that I had a four-year-old son. I thought about the offer and felt that it might be the only chance I would ever have for my dream to come true. I was very excited and wrote back. I let them know that I would love to come to America. I also told them about Michael for the first time. I hadn't told them about him because my birth mother and I had no real relationship and I didn't think she would care.

I wasn't sure that the Deutsche Demokratische Republik (DDR) government would let this happen because its' official policy was not to let anyone of working age leave the country. With all of my fears, though, I was still hanging on to my dream.

One day a notice from the post office to pick up a certified letter was on my door. I had no idea of what it could be and I was shocked to see the sender. It was from the American Embassy in Berlin. My heart started beating. My hands were shaking and I couldn't open it fast enough. The ambassador asked me to come to see him in person, because he needed to speak with me. "Michael, would you like to come with Mama for a long train ride?"

"Yes, Mama."

"We're going to the big city to see a very important man." We arrived after a long ride at 2:30 a.m. in Berlin and checked into a hotel for some rest. The next morning as I looked out of the hotel window I could see the Wall. It had barbed wire on top and it was about 50 feet away. Freedom was so close, yet so far away. Just on the other side of that wall. In that moment, how I wished I were a bird. How sad to see such a beautiful city divided, knowing that on the other side there were also Germans. It was very heartbreaking for me. That same morning after breakfast, I called a taxi to take us to the embassy. It was a large, old building, with cars from many different nations and soldiers in American uniforms. What impressed me the most was the flag, the Stars and Stripes. After showing a guard soldier my letter we were escorted inside. I felt so special that I had to pinch myself to see if it was real.

Michael was also very excited, "Mama do you see the big cars? Mama do you see the soldiers with big guns? Mama here, Mama there!"

"Yes, I see Michael, these soldiers protect us from the bad people." I was very nervous, I tried to concentrate on saying the right words. I had a hard time keeping Michael still, and I said to him, "Listen Michael, do you remember what Mama told you? Behave and be a good boy because being here is very important."

"Yes Mama, I'll be good."

The soldier stopped in front of a big door and knocked. A lady opened it and asked who we were and then said, "The Ambassador is expecting you, please come in." A man with silver gray hair and a smile pointed to a big leather chair and said, "Please have a seat, and welcome to my office."

I sat next to a very large American flag on a pole; this was the closest I had ever been to my dream. I was showered with goose bumps and tears rolled out of my eyes, it was a very overwhelming and powerful moment for me. I touched the flag with my hands for the first time in my life. Staring at the flag I could only wish that one day I would live proudly under its symbol of freedom.

After a long conversation with the Ambassador, he said to me, "I have papers from the white house signed by President Carter which are in response to a letter written by your stepfather, asking for your release from the DDR. I can't promise you anything, but I'll do everything in my power to help you and your son. The East German Government will make the final decision. We will have to be patient and wait, this won't be the last time we will see each other." He took us to the door, shook our hands and said "Auf Wiedersehn."

I couldn't believe it; I had just spoken to the official representative of the United States. It was all like a dream. We had plenty of time before the train ride back home. I tried to relax but it wasn't easy. I thought about my vacation in this city over 16 years ago. As we came close to the Brandenburg Gate, I saw the wall again. I saw armed soldiers' watchtowers and the areas where the buried land mines were hidden under the soil. Sadness came over me once again. Families were separated, not allowed to see each other or even talk. Phone lines were disconnected from the east side to the west side.

Michael asked, "Why are you crying Mama? And what is that thing over there, it looks so ugly?"

"It's a concrete wall and it makes Mama very sad. One day when you are old enough to understand, Mama will tell you a story about this ugly wall." I gave him a big hug and we went to the train station. I had lots of time to think about our future on our train ride home.

A few weeks later we went back to Berlin. The Ambassador said, "Be patient, things don't look that bad, don't give up your dream." "If I have some news I will let you know." I was waiting and waiting but it became silent. I didn't hear anything from the Embassy or my stepfather. It seemed like everyone forgot about us and the whole world had turned against us. Was this the end of my hope, would I ever reach the top of the mountain? Would my dream come true? During this time of uncertainty, I was determined to hold on tightly to my dream and not let it slip away.

Shortly after I moved into my new apartment, I invited an old friend to visit. He had escaped to West Germany before the border was closed. I felt comfortable having company because I had new furniture and the place looked cozy. Every visitor who came from the West had to check in and out of the local police station. The next day after my friend arrived, someone knocked on my door. It was a tenant who lived on the first floor, and to my knowledge he was one of those brainwashed Red Bulls. He invited himself into my apartment looking around suspiciously and said, "I hear you have a visitor from West Germany. I need to talk to him, and by the way I have been instructed to spend some time everyday in your apartment."

I was very angry and said to him, "Are you spying on me, is it a crime to have a guest, haven't you ever heard anything about privacy? I am asking you to leave and not come back."

He was upset; "I will have to report you about this incident."

I became even angrier and started yelling, "Leave me alone and get out of here." That son of a bitch had some nerve and came back the next day, but I didn't open the door. This was such an embarrassing situation to have happened because of my friend. He was in shock and couldn't believe what had just happened, all he said was, "Damn Communism."

For me to call the police wouldn't do any good, they had probably put the tenant up to it. They stuck their ugly noses in everything; the government even dictated people's private lives.

Silence is Golden

I was sad and disappointed. I became very depressed and began to isolate myself, and stopped talking to my co-workers and friends. There was nobody I could trust, talk to or ask for advice. I had to make decisions and prayed that I would make the right ones. The secret I carried was like a ticking bomb inside me. I was all alone and wanted it that way.

"What's the matter with you?" everybody asked.

"Nothing," I answered.

My friend sitting next to me at the work station asked "Gitta, are you mad at me? Did I upset you?"

"No, I'm not mad at you, it's my problem and one day you'll understand."

One Friday, right after lunch, the president of the company called me into his office and said to me, "The police station called, they want to see you at 2 pm. Are you in some kind of trouble?"

I got very nervous; I knew somebody was always watching me. Even the Ambassador warned me to be careful and keep everything to myself. I had a bad feeling when I went to the police station. A very grumpy looking and unfriendly officer said, "We have some information about you, you're trying to leave this country."

I played stupid and said, "I don't know what you are talking about."

"You know what I mean, and if you don't stop it, I can put you in jail and you won't see your boy anymore. His name is Michael, right?"

I knew he wasn't kidding. I was very scared but tried not to show my fear and stay calm. My biggest concern was my little boy. I couldn't cry out for help in order to get out of this situation. I told myself to be strong; it's now or never.

I told the officer that I had connections to very important people, and they would be interested in my story. I was bluffing, I really didn't have any connections but this really woke him up

He jumped up from his chair, his face close to mine and yelled, "What connections are you talking about, and who are these people?"

I tried to stay calm and answered, "You have your secrets and I have mine." He screamed at me and told me to get out of his office as he reached for the phone.

As I was leaving, I turned around and said with a smile, "One day I'll be back."

"Get out of here," he yelled, "Get out of my face." Then he smashed the door behind me.

I don't know how I got the courage; they were able to destroy people's lives. Lots of thoughts went through my mind, if they put me in jail, what would happen to Michael? Scared to death, I could only wait and wait some more, fearing the unknown; it was very tense and nerve racking.

After several months I got a letter from Berlin. The American Ambassador asked me to come immediately; he had good news for me. I took Michael, jumped on the next express train to Berlin. The Ambassador said, "good to see you again, we are making some progress and maybe you will be able to leave the country. *We've traded computers for you.* From our side, everything is ready, and by the way here is $400 dollars your stepfather sent to you. Now we are just waiting for an okay from the East German government. Don't do anything until you hear from me again."

I was so nervous and excited that I wanted to scream, but it was not over yet, anything could still happen.

About six weeks later, I got another call at work; this time it was the police chief who wanted to see me. Living all this time in fear, my first thought was that this was it; they are going to lock me up. Maybe I pushed them to far. The chief was waiting for me; he locked the door behind me, and even closed the blinds. I was scared as I waited for the bad news. I pictured myself, locked up in a prison cell with only water and bread. According to communist law, I would be a political prisoner. I would pay a big price for trying to be free. And what about my son? I was watching the chief, who just stared at me with a pale face.

I couldn't take the pressure anymore and I asked, "Sir, you wanted to see me?"

He didn't respond, just shuffled through a bunch of papers in front of him. Shaking his head, he finally said, "This paper is telling me a story about a mother and her little boy, and how they can leave this country. It also tells me their names, Brigitte and Michael."

First I wanted to say, "You bastard, don't play games with me." But instead said, "That's a funny joke."

He said, "I'm not joking, this is a very serious situation, you and your son can leave, I have all the papers ready." It hit me suddenly, I felt sick, and saw his angry and white face. Then I lost the ground under my feet. After I came out of it, I wanted to scream, but my throat was all tensed up. He gave me some papers and said, "I have to ask you for your ID card and you will have to leave this country by the last day of April. Now you are nobody, with no country and no identification."

I answered, "This is the best thing anyone has ever said to me," and I left. I never forgot his look, full of hatred and jealously. He looked like he wanted to kill me. If looks could kill I would've dropped dead right there.

Before I left the police station, I went to visit the grumpy officer who had spoken to me the first time. I had to, because I promised him that "I would be back." I knocked on the door, entered his office, and waved the papers I had just gotten in front of his face. Before he could say anything, I said with a huge smile and a very confident feeling, "I told you I would be back."

His face was priceless; he yelled at me and called me a crazy woman. I went outside, took a deep breath and yelled, "The hell with all of you, the hell with Communism, I'm free."

As I reached for a cigarette, people looked at me like I was crazy, but what did I care? I was shaking, crying and laughing; this couldn't be real. It was have been a dream too nice to be true, just so unbelievable. On that day I was riding my bike to work, but I was so excited that I couldn't' ride it home, so I pushed it all through the city. I picked up my son at the kindergarten and said to the girls, "Today was Michaels' last day."

Before they started to ask questions, we were out the door. I had to hold back my emotions, but the moment that I opened the door to my new apartment, where I had just moved to a few months ago, I let it all out. I started screaming, jumping, singing, crying and hugging Michael. "We're free, we're going to America."

He just looked at me like he didn't understand what I was saying, with his eyes wide open he asked, "Are you okay Mama?"

"Yes son, I'm okay, I have never felt better." What a day it was, it would change our lives forever. What the future would bring us, only time would tell.

It's show time and I was ready to blow off some steam. With nothing to lose, I went to work late on purpose. My boss came to me and yelled, "You're late."

"No, I'm early."

He yelled even more and became angrier. "I need an explanation."

It felt good talking back to him, playing this little game. I said to him, "I don't have to give you any excuse!" I hated him, he was so brainwashed that it made me sick. He never liked me because of my attitude and always picked on me. I just ignored him, went to my workstation and started cleaning up for good. I took a big trash can and began to smash one glass after another, while yelling "yippy, yi yeah." My friend who was sitting next to me jumped from the chair and ran. Everybody looked at me like I had lost it. My boss didn't know what to do, and ran to the president of the company for help.

He came to me and said, "What is going on here, come in my office right now! What's the matter with you? I have never seen you behave like this, if you don't apologize I will have to fire you."

"That's not necessary, I quit right now."

"You have to give a two week notice, its company policy."

"The hell with your policy, it's not made for me, I quit right now and there is nothing you can do about it." We had a little fire going, but as we both cooled down, I said to him, "Okay, I'll give you an explanation. Believe it or not, I am going to America and nothing else matters anymore."

The next moment the brainwashed boss opened the door and tried to come in, he probably thought he could take care of the situation.

"What is it?" the President asked. "Please leave and close the door behind you, I can handle this without you."

"Thank you," I said, "I don't want him snooping around me."

He smiled and said, "I am sorry for this interruption."

"It's okay."

He sat back into his chair and asked, "So, you are going to America?"

"Yes sir, remember the phone call I had yesterday? That's when I got the good news."

"It's impossible, I don't believe it."

"That's not my problem."

"I'm going to find out because the police chief is a friend of mine." He dialed the number on the phone while he looked at me. As he talked he looked surprised, then hung up. "It's unbelievable, you told me the truth."

"I have no reason to lie to you," I said. We always liked each other; he was not as brainwashed as the others.

"I've known you for many years, you have always been an outsider with a western attitude. Now it looks like you have gotten you way. You don't fit in this society, that for sure."

"I never tried, sir. I'm sorry I got so carried away at the beginning of our conversation."

"I am sorry too. So that's it, you're not coming back, you're leaving us? You're a very hard worker with a lot of talent, and you have done a lot of good things for this company. I wish you good luck and I will miss you. But if you come back one day, you can have your job back."

"I appreciate your offer sir, but that day will never come. Thank you sir." He gave me a hug and I left his office. I went back to my workstation and finished what I started, cleaning up.

The news spread like a wild fire. Everybody stopped what he or she was doing, except one, and I don't have to say whom. They were all in shock, wondering how I did this. Most of them would have liked to come with me, but they never tried hard enough. Bill, the one with the jeans, came and said, "You son of a gun, you did it. You have more courage than the rest of us."

My friend who sat at the station next to me started crying and hugging me. "I can't believe it, now I understand why you acted so strangely. I would have done the same."

"I told you, one day you will understand."

"Yes, now I do. I was worried about you and was afraid you were going crazy."

I had done the unthinkable; no one was allowed to leave the country legally. Only the retired elderly were allowed to leave because they couldn't contribute to the workforce; the government didn't care about them. If they decided to leave the government would not pay them their retirement benefits. The next day I went back to say goodbye, it was bittersweet. I gave everybody something: beer for the boys, wine and coffee for the office people and a bottle of Champagne for the President. Having known most of them for many years, it was hard to say goodbye. However, I had big plans ahead of me and I had to move forward with my life.

CHAPTER X

Escape

Slowly I regained my faith, but my mind and body were in a trance. There was so much running around to do; going places to fill out papers, cancellations, city hall and much more. By the end of the day Michael and I were exhausted. But I could go to the moon if I had to, just to get out of there. The road to freedom got closer and closer and made me stronger. I remembered what the Ambassador told me, that they would probably take everything from me except the clothes on my back and jewelry you are wearing. That was good to know, I went to the bank, closed out my account and went shopping for jewelry.

By East German standards I bought very expensive items. "Did you rob a bank?" the clerk asked.

"No, much better, I hit the jackpot, I'm going to America." Nobody took me seriously; it was too unbelievable for them to accept. Then I began to wonder how I would smuggle the $400 U.S. dollars I had and how I would take them across the border. There must be a way I thought, "But how?" After my Mama passed away, I started smoking. I sat at the table with four $100 dollar bills in front of me; I lit my cigarette and stared at the money. All of a sudden an idea clicked in my head. Being creative and skilled with my hands and fingers I used my skills. With tweezers I began to pull the tobacco out the cigarette and rolled the bills into the same shape and put them carefully back into the paper. On one end was the filter and the other end was the tobacco. I laid one of the cigarettes next to the special one and compared them. Bingo! I got it; it was perfect, mission accomplished. Now they would not find the money. I put them back into the pack with the others and kept them in a special place.

Michael also had to go to the hospital for shots, the ones required for entering the United States. When we talk about having a bad day, this was not a good one for him. The moment he saw a needle he freaked out. He became hysterical, started to kick, cry and lay on the floor. It took two nurses and me to calm him down. During the hustle and bustle one of the nurses gave him the shots and before he realized it, it was all over. Although when I was holding him in my arms to comfort him, he was still shaking and crying. After a while he said, "Mama, I don't want a shot, I'm scared."

"You don't have to be scared anymore because you just got them."

He was surprised and answered, "Oh really, I didn't feel anything."

Time was running out, I had to get rid of all my stuff and clean out the apartment. Everything had to go. I gave it all to my friends and neighbors for free, because I was not allowed to take anything with me. But for me it was all worth it, to get out of there and be free.

As things started moving out the door of the apartment, Frank came to see his son. He had no idea what was going on and asked, "Where are you? You're never home. And what is this all about, you just moved in."

"You're right, and now I'm moving out." For the first time I told him that we were leaving; we were going to America.

His chin dropped, mouth and eyes wide open, he yelled, "No way, that's impossible, how can that be? And you're not taking the boy."

"What kind of mother do you think I am? I'm not leaving without him. Where I am going, he is going. This boy brightens up my life, we belong together and nothing can separate us, not even you."

This little child, so innocent and cute, with his curly brown hair, is everything to me. Whenever I had problems or was in pain, I would take him in my arms and everything went away. He was like magic and the best medicine for me. I was angry with Frank and said, "You've got you're nerve telling me what to do. Why do you care all of a sudden? You're never around and we will be just fine without you."

He was running back and forth in the almost empty apartment. He stepped in front of Michael and asked, "Michael, do you want to stay with Papa?"

Michael turned around looked at me and said, "I am going with Mama, I want to be a cowboy and drive big cars."

"Listen Frank, I don't have time to argue with you, I have to pack and have lots of things to take care of."

He was angry, and before he left he said, "We will see, you won't get away with this so easily. I am going to my lawyer, you're not taking the boy."

"Good luck, I'll send you a post card so you know we are there." That was the last time we saw each other and the last time Michael saw his father. I never did send him that post card.

As the world kept turning, so was my age. It was hard to believe how fast the years flew by. I reached the age of 37 and my son just turned five; Mama had left me eleven years ago. The last day of April was coming soon. I was so ready, ready like never before for what lay ahead of me. The hunger for freedom made me strong, I felt like I could move mountains. I went to the train station in the next big city, made reservations buying the most expensive tickets I could get. If I left this place that I hated so much, I was going to go out in style. First class.

Three days later I called a taxi to take us to the station. Some of my friends came to say goodbye; we all cried, wondering if we would ever see each other again. As the train started moving, they waved with their tissues and shouted, "Send us a post card from Hollywood." I promised them I would.

After some time on the train, we came closer to the West German border. I was so nervous I smoked one cigarette after another. Soldiers with guns were everywhere; watchtowers, fences and invisible land mines in no-mans' land. I realized that it wouldn't be over until we were on the other side. The train moved very slowly and then came to a stop. This was the last checkpoint on the East side. My heart was pounding and I prayed, "Please God, don't let anything bad happen, we are so close to freedom." A lady in uniform with a mean face asked for my passport. Not having one, I showed her my papers instead. She looked at them, never having seen anything like them and disappeared. After a short while, she returned with a man in uniform with even a longer look on his face. They ordered me to empty my suitcase and bag. After searching everything they looked at me like I had come from another planet. "It's okay," the man said, so I got my papers back. My nerves almost exploded, and after they left I reached for another cigarette.

Slowly the train started moving again, the soldiers and towers disappeared, but I was not sure if we had crossed the border. Then I saw houses and cars that were so nice and clean that I realized that we were on free soil. I started jumping, yelling and screaming, dancing all over and shouting, "We made it, we made it, thank God we are free." I opened the window from the train, took a deep breath and filled my lungs with the air of freedom. I can't describe how I felt in that moment, it was too overwhelming. Some elderly people came to look at what was going on because of the noise I was making. After I told them my story, some had tears in their eyes, and said, "Welcome to the Free World, welcome to West Germany."

I had some cigarettes left and looked for the hidden money, but to my surprise they were gone. I was such a nervous wreck that I smoked them without realizing it. I couldn't believe it after all my hard work at hiding the money, it was gone. Four hundred dollars had gone up in smoke. But for me it was just paper, and no amount of money in this world could pay for being free, it was priceless.

For three weeks we stayed at my stepfathers' mothers' house. I felt very sick from the stress of the journey; all the stress of my new reality was beginning to kick in. It was like a dream, simply unbelievable. People came from the newspapers and TV channels offering me good money for an interview. Everybody wanted to know how it was possible to leave the Iron Curtain. They talked about us in the news; how two people legally left East Germany. It was all over the news; I don't know how they found out so fast. I was so exhausted and to shy too talk to the public about it. I probably became famous for a short time, but it was not for me. It was enough just to deal with the reality of being in the free world.

I tried to calm down and relax; the first week we didn't really go anywhere. Michael would sit in front of the house all day long watching the cars go by. Sometimes I would sit next to him and I felt like a kid in a candy store. People were laughing and so friendly over there. My stepfather's mom took us to all the nice stores, filled with nice clothes, fruit and many other things we had never seen before. It felt like being in paradise; it was like heaven on earth. Everyday we enjoyed being in the free world; it was so different from where we had come from, like day and night. It was unbelievable and my dream to be free had become true.

For many years I had been waiting for this day to come. Now it was time for this very special event. My stepfather sent money for the airline tickets.

I went to the travel agency and asked, "I would like to have two tickets to Los Angeles, nonstop one way."

"You're not coming back?" the lady asked. She showed me on a big map hanging on the wall and said, "From Frankfort you will fly over Holland, and then just water, followed by Iceland and Greenland. Then you will fly over the Rocky Mountains to Los Angeles."

"That's a long way."

"Yes it is," she replied.

I'll never forget that day; it was Thursday June 4th 1977. The flight was scheduled at 1:50 p.m. from Frankfurt to Los Angeles. We rode in a special train that took us directly to the airport. I had flown before, but to make sure I didn't get sick, I took some motion sickness pills. I didn't want to miss a thing and see the world from above. Here we were, flying through the unknown to a country we had never seen before. I didn't have one penny in my wallet, just a suitcase, handbag and didn't speak the language and my little boy by my side not knowing what was waiting for us. When we took off in the big bird, I had mixed feelings; I was sad and happy at the same time. I was leaving my homeland, maybe forever. Now some people probably think that flying is no big deal, but for us it would change our lives forever.

Many thoughts came into my head. We had so many new obstacles to overcome; language, strange people, a land and culture we didn't know. What was waiting for us, would we survive? I was scared, but this was our new reality, the one I had dreamed about for so many years. And what about my son? I did most of this for him. As quickly as all my thoughts came they disappeared. Maybe my brain and nerves were playing games with me.

For Michael it was the first time on a plane. He was so excited, running all over the place. After a while I didn't see Michael, so I asked the flight attendant to help me find him. Michael's curiosity guided him to the cockpit of the Boeing 747. I followed the flight attendant up the stairs to the first-class area and the cockpit. There I saw a man with a cowboy hat, boots on the table and papers all around him. He must have been a rich cowboy, I thought.

Then I heard the attendant say in German, "Boy, you are not allowed to be here, this is the cockpit." There was Michael, sitting on the Captain's lap and asking him questions about the instruments.

"Michael, what are you doing here?"

"It's okay," the Captain said with a smile "but now you'll have to go back to your seat because I have to do my job. I'm going to fly you to America." I think the attendant was more embarrassed than I but I apologized to him. The plane was big, a Lufthansa 747 Jumbo Jet. We had a window seat so I had a chance to see everything below us. I felt like a queen in the sky, being on top of the world. Free like a bird and on the way to my dreamland. This was so overwhelming and wonderful; it could not get better than this. This was reality and nothing could stand in our way. Two young German men sat in front of us and started a conversation with me. They ordered some drinks and asked me if I would like to have one.

As nervous as I was, and not having any money, I said, "Yes, thank you, I think I need one." I told them my situation, that I didn't speak English.

"Don't worry, we'll help you when you arrive."

I kept looking nervously at my watch. My heart started beating faster, as I looked down I saw mountains covered with snow. At that moment, the attendant's voice came over the radio and announced that we were flying over the Rocky Mountains.

A little while later I heard the Captain say, "Ladies and Gentlemen, please fasten your seatbelts, we will be landing in Los Angeles shortly."

I felt a shower of goose bumps all over my body, butterflies in my stomach, my heart was jumping through my throat and my nerves were ready to explode. The two gentlemen sitting by us told me to stay close by and they would show us where to go. It was a smooth landing and as we left the airplane, my feet felt like jelly. The moment I stood on American soil, I went down on my knees and kissed the ground. With tears of joy I sobbed like a baby. At that moment I felt like the luckiest and richest girl on the whole planet. I was floating on a cloud from heaven. "Thank God, we are in America. We are free!" It was amazing how far away from home my dream had brought us.

As we came to the luggage checkout, a man said in German, "I can't believe it, you came from East Germany? I've been working at this airport for 28 years and I've never seen anyone come from there. You don't have to open your luggage, anyone coming from East Germany has nothing to bring." This man had come from Berlin and said with a big smile, "Welcome to America and good luck."

CHAPTER XI

Our New World

Our arrival in America was not as smooth at I thought it would be, some unexpected situations occurred. My birthmothers' husband, who I never met, called us in Germany before we left and told me, "We're coming to pick you up at the airport." I wasn't sure if I would remember my biological mother since I had not seen here in over 23 years. I was looking around when somebody patted me on my shoulder and said, "Gitta." She introduced me to her husband.

He took Michael and hugged him." You and Grandpa are going to have lots of fun." He looked at me and said, "Welcome to America, it's nice to see you and the boy."

But I had no welcome from her; she stood there like an iceberg. I knew she was unhappy to see us, I could feel it, and it would become more obvious later. The first step outside the airport welcomed us with blue skies. It felt so good feeling the warm sun on our skin as the palm trees waved in a light breeze. It was like the palms were saying, "welcome to California." Then we went to the parking lot. Her husband opened the car door for us his car.

"What a nice big car you have."

"Yes, and we have another one just like it at home."

I couldn't believe it. He had two nice cars and this was unheard of in the DDR. We drove on the freeway for about forty minutes to their house. It was very nice, with its' own swimming pool. I had only seen places like it in the movies. We were exhausted from our journey, when we sat on the couch; there were glasses and a bottle of Champagne.

Her husband said, "We need to make a toast. Today is a very special day. Prost. Welcome to America."

We were tired from the emotions, travel and hot climate. My first night was a sleepless one; it was all too much to deal with. The next day my birthmother wanted us to sit at the pool with her. I felt like I was getting sick, saw stars and started vomiting. So did Michael. The temperature by the pool was 102 degrees. I remembered the doctor saying to me in Germany, "Your blood is thick from living in a cold climate, it will take at least 2 years to adapt to a new climate. Madam (my birth mother) didn't care much about us; she insisted that we sit with her at the pool so she could get a tan.

The second day she took us to the market. The heat was bothering us, and when we went into the store, I became even sicker. My eyes almost popped out of my head. I had never seen so many nice things in a market, and in the fruit and vegetable section my chest started hurting and I started to cry. It was unbelievable; so many beautiful things to see. I had seen some nice stores in West Germany, but nothing like this. I didn't want to think about the markets we used to have in East Germany. They were so small, ugly and empty.

My birthmother's husband told me one day, "If you like, you can call me Dad and Michael can call me Opi (Grandpa)."

In my whole life I never had anyone I could Dad, now I was feeling uncomfortable. Did I want to call a stranger Dad? After all I had just met him? Besides, I was thirty-seven years old, it just didn't seem right to me. I wasn't ready for that, and asked him, "If that's okay with you, can I call you Opi like Michael does?"

"Sure, if that makes you more comfortable, I don't mind."

I was relieved at how easily we resolved the situation. But our agreement backfired; Christel, my birthmother didn't allow it. She got really nasty and started yelling. One thing I could say is that it was very embarrassing being yelled at in front of my son. She was not acting like the lady she pretended to be.

One day Opi came in with a big smile and said, "I took two weeks' vacation just for the two of you. I'll show you all of California and take you to all the sights." Michael and I were looking forward to the trip. He has been car crazy since he was a baby. Seeing all the cars on the freeways was too much for him. He was so excited that he went pee in his pants because he didn't have time to go to the bathroom. Opi never had children of his own. He was so nice to Michael. It made me feel good. He took us to the beaches, amusement parks, Hollywood and other nice places. Sometimes a friend of his came along. One time we went to Mexico, then to Canada. I was scared to death, all my life I had lived around walls and borders; we could pass with one or two questions and that was it. For me this was a big surprise, it was so easy to cross a border.

What was wrong with the picture where we came from? We were now living in a free world and it was time to get used to it. What a wonderful feeling it was to have freedom. I couldn't get enough of it and soaked up every moment of it.

Sometimes Christel would come along, but it seemed like she wasn't enjoying anything. "Why are we going here? I've been here before." One time I heard her say, "Honey, you're spending too much money on them." She didn't work, she stayed at home lying by the pool, or looking in the mirror like Snow White. Opi had a very good job in a high paying position and gave her lots of comforts. On the kitchen counter, there was always a big bowl with all kinds of fruit. For us, things such as fresh fruit were a luxury that we had never had in East Germany.

One day Michael reached out for a peach, and as he was ready to take a bite, Christel began to yell at him and take the peach away. "You only take things after you ask me, didn't your Mama teach you manners?" Little Michael started to cry.

I was very angry, "Yes, I taught him manners, but he's just a little boy. What do you know about raising kids? Besides, he's never eaten a peach before." After this she was quiet because she knew I was right.

One day she sent me to walk her dog, a little poodle named Blackie. Usually Michael came along, but not that day. He was busy playing with a toy car that Opi had given him. As I came home from the walk, I heard Michael crying. He came running to me and said, "Look Mama what she did!" as he pulled his pants down. I saw a big red spot with five-finger marks on his skin. I was very angry, went to her and asked, "Why did you hurt Michael? I can see the finger marks on his butt. To make marks like this, you must have hit him very hard."

She started yelling, "He broke one of my plants with his stupid car."

I said to her, "I don't want you to hurt Michael ever again. If somebody will punish him, it will be me."

Now she became hysterical and yelled even more. "Don't you come here and tell me what to do, this is my house. If you don't like it here, why don't you go back to where you came from? I didn't want you here in the first place."

"I know that, you have given me that feeling everyday." I didn't like to raise my voice, not to my boy or anyone else, but she hurt my feelings and it made me angry. "I don't know who you are, but you are a very selfish person with no feelings for others. You never cared for me all of my life, and I can never call you my mother. You could be nice to Michael, but instead you are mean and you abuse him. What's the matter with you; what kind of person are you? If you hurt my son, you are also hurting me, and I'll make sure you never hurt him again."

Opi came home from work; usually Michael would run to him shouting "Opi is here, Opi is here," but that afternoon he lay on the bed crying instead. Opi called "Where is my boy, how come he is not yelling Opi is here?"

She walked outside and said to her husband, "Your boy was bad today, very bad."

Before she could say more, I said to Opi, "Come, I would like to show you something." Michael was lying on the bed with an icepack and crying. I pulled his pants down.

"Oh my god, who did this?"

"Not me, who else lives in the house?"

He went to his wife while I closed the door and stayed in another room with Michael. Then I heard yelling.

After a while Opi came to us and said, "This won't happen again, I promise."

"Opi, Opi, that hurt," Michael said.

"I know, my boy, Opi is here and everything will be okay." He tried to cheer Michael up and after a while they both became silly. I was still upset and told him what happened earlier that day, and what his wife said to me. "Maybe we should leave, it doesn't seem like it will work out." But there was another big problem, we didn't speak a word of English and I didn't have a job.

"Why don't we wait a little more?"

"We have to do something soon, because Michael is very scared of her." We talked to her only if we had to. There was something else she did to me; it was very disgusting. After she went in the bathtub, she called us. "It's your turn now to take a bath." We had to go in the same water she had cleaned herself with; we were not good enough to use clean water. It was very humiliating. When I questioned her about it, she said, "We have to save water because it is so expensive."

We weren't happy staying at this house. The way she treated us. Always putting us down, never having anything nice to say. Opi was the exact opposite of her. He was understanding, patient and taught us how to live American style. He was a man with a big heart who we appreciated very much. There was no one else who would have helped us.

One warm night, we were sitting by the pool with candles burning and drinking wine. Opi liked it, it was a good time to relax, and he taught Michael how to swim.

One day Christel did something else which was even more shocking. Michael was playing outside with Blackie and I was sitting in the guest room writing letters to friends. All of a sudden I heard Michael yelling "Mommy, Mommy," as he opened the door with a disturbed expression on his face.

I was worried and asked him "What's the matter? Are you okay?"

"She is naked, she is naked," he said.

"Who is," I asked.

"Grandma is, in the pool."

"What are you talking about, nobody is naked."

"Yes Mommy, look." He pointed to the pool.

Michael was right; I couldn't believe my eyes. I was shocked. That was too much, how could she do this in front of my little boy? She wasn't only swimming, but also lounging around in her chair totally naked. For me this was very difficult to explain to Michael. Didn't she feel ashamed to expose herself in front of her own grandchild? I was angry; I realized how selfish and hurtful she could be to others. But not to make the tense situation worse, I decided not to say a word. Besides, I was only a guest in her home.

Two days later she had the nerve to tell me that we should all walk around naked in the house.

I couldn't believe what I heard and said, "I don't think so. I was raised the old fashioned way, my son has never seen me without clothes, and if that's the way it's going to be, you're asking too much."

She didn't like my answer, and from that day on I made sure that Michael wasn't around when she went swimming. He was afraid of her; I had no respect for her and the distance between us grew wider and wider. I felt she was mentally and physically abusive, and had to protect my son from it. I knew from my own experience how painful and damaging this can be. I couldn't tolerate her behavior, it was unacceptable. For me the only way to escape this uneasy situation was to move out, but this was easier said than done.

Some time later Opi said to Christel, "I have an idea, why don't we have a party for Gitta and Michael at our house."

"But honey, that costs lots of money."

"Don't worry, I'll take care of it. Christel, I want you to send an invitation to all of our friends, you take care of the food and I'll take care of the drinks." She was the kind of person to show off with nice expensive clothes and glitter. I knew she was embarrassed by what I was wearing, and said to her husband, "Honey, we need to buy some nice clothes for the kids."

"Okay, here is my credit card. Please take them shopping."

The next day she took us to a big department store, and we watched her pick out and buy clothes for herself. She didn't ask us if we wanted anything. The only thing she bought for Michael was a pair of jeans and a shirt.

"But what about me?" I was thinking, "Didn't Opi say to buy things for the kids?" I was upset about the situation, but shut my mouth because at least my son got a few things he needed. When we came home that day, she opened the closet door and showed me some of her older dresses. She asked me which one I liked.

"I'm okay, I don't need anything. Thank you very much."

When Opi came home after work, he asked Christel, "Did you go shopping today? Show me what you bought."

"I have a pair of jeans and a shirt for Michael, wait, I will show them to you."

"That's very nice, what did you get for Gitta?"

"Oh, she didn't like what we looked at."

I was very upset by her lies, but instead I said, "Its okay Opi, I'm okay." I saw a change in his face.

With an angry voice he said, "You don't like the clothes we have here in America, what's the matter with you?"

I was embarrassed, I had hurt his feelings, and without telling him how the shopping trip went I said, "I just don't want you to spend money for me, you have already done so much for us."

The day of the party finally arrived on a Saturday. About thirty people came, everybody was dressed in style and they were very friendly. Michael was wearing his new outfit and he looked cute in it. I was wearing one of Christel's. We were introduced to everybody; we talked, danced and had a nice evening. Some people went for a swim or sat around the pool. I didn't feel very comfortable; most people spoke German, but even so, this many people around me made me nervous. Everything was fine until disaster struck.

Christel was so drunk she kept falling over, yelling and screaming at the guests and us, and was kissing every man who came near her. Opi tried to calm her down, but she slapped him in the face in front of all of their friends.

After that the guests began to leave, they had seen enough. I was so embarrassed; I grabbed Michael and locked the door to our bedroom.

After a while, I heard Opi knocking and asking me for my help. "We have to take her to bed." I saw her lying on the floor passed out. As we carried her into the bedroom, she was vomiting. The next morning, the house looked like a bomb had gone off. Broken glasses everywhere; alcohol on the carpet, flowers on the floor and a broken lamp. It took us almost all of that Sunday to clean up the house.

I said to Opi, "I don't want to live here anymore, it's not good for Michael to see all of this. Help me find a place and a job."

"But what about the language, how can you work without speaking English?"

"I don't know, I'll make it one way or another."

Finally after a month we moved out of the house. While the doors at Opi's were closing, new doors were opening for us. We were looking for a fresh start. This had not been the nicest of times so I was happy to leave them behind me. I couldn't let one individual person destroy my hopes and dreams. We had come to America with nothing, and everything we gained in this new country was a new experience.

Opi found a nice apartment in town for us. We had nothing, only a suitcase. Opi gave us his old refrigerator, a mattress and blankets. That's how we lived for about six months. "A refrigerator you must have because of the hot climate." He sure looked out for us. Every other day he brought us food and we discussed what to do next.

"I need a job, I can't depend on you all the time," I said. My biggest concern was Michael; I couldn't leave him alone. To ask Christel to take care of him wasn't an option. I wouldn't be able to work, because I would be worried about what she might do to him. And besides, I am sure she would probably not do it anyway. What did she know about raising a child?

Opi had a solution; he offered to pay for Michael to go to day care while I worked. We went to sign up for Michael, but two days later the lady said to Opi, "I am sorry we can't help your son, he can't speak or understand English." Opi was very upset with the lady, and after a heated debate, the lady said he could stay. He was scared and cried everyday when I picked him up. I wasn't very happy about seeing him upset and unhappy, but I had no other choice at that time. Shortly after that I started a job in an electronics company. It was hard and discouraging for me. First of all, I had never done this before, and secondly, I had a language barrier. It was very hard and frustrating. Whatever they said to me, I couldn't understand one word. I just watched the girl next to me and tried to copy her. If somebody told me to do something I could only give him or her a puzzled look.

Many times they would call a German girl from a different department to translate. I felt stupid and helpless and cried everyday. But I decided that "I have to learn this language no matter what," and Michael became my teacher. As we all know kids pick up a language very quickly and can learn more than one at the same time. Everyday, Michael taught me another English word, and it began to work. Slowly I could understand and say a few words.

I wanted to be independent, and I promised myself we would make it. I worked very hard at a job that I didn't enjoy. But it helped support us and allowed us to survive. Before we came to America I had earned my International drivers license but it wasn't accepted in California. I was unhappy about it, but my English wasn't good enough to pass the test. Opi would give me his car to drive and for months I drove around without a license.

"You have to get used to this traffic," he said.

I knew I could get into big trouble by doing this, but it was an emergency situation. I improved at my new electronic assembly job; I was good with my fingers and put out high quality work. Little Michael's English was now almost as good as his German, which was a big step forward for both of us.

After awhile I began to study for my driver's license examination. I studied, but there were still many words I didn't understand, but I wanted to try anyway. I was very disappointed when I failed my first test. "Well maybe I will do better next time I thought."

One day Opi said, "I have to renew my driver's license. Are you ready for yours?"

"I don't know, maybe I will wait a little longer."

He went to take it and failed. I studied very hard and a few weeks later, scared and nervous, I went back to try again. After I returned the test papers, I heard the lady say, "You passed, congratulations." That was a big surprise and relief for me. As I was driving home I was very proud. To every car that passed me on the freeway I would yell, "I did it, I did it," but it seemed like I was the only one who cared.

When I arrived at home Opi asked, "Did you or did you not?"

And very proudly I answered, "Yes I did it, I passed."

"That's wonderful, all you need now is a car and you're all set. I'm very proud of you."

"I know, but the problem is that I don't have the money to buy one." This was a happy day for me because I did it all by myself and it meant a lot to me. Now I didn't have to worry anymore about breaking the law, I could sleep better at night. I have always been honest in my life, and felt guilty about breaking the law. But there was no excuse for doing it; I was very lucky to not get busted. Shame on me.

The apartment started looking nicer, Opi go us a used couch and bed, and some neighbors gave us a table, chairs and dishes. I was able to pay the rent by working overtime. We enjoyed everyday not having someone around us who would not give us a hard time and try to run our lives. I even had a telephone for the first time in my life; it was a big luxury for me.

One day Opi came by to see how we were doing, "Let's sit on the patio, it's such a nice day. Look at the blue car parked on the street, let's go down and check it out."

As we looked at the car, I noticed that it was in good condition and very clean.

Then he reached into his pocket and gave me a key. "Let's go for a ride, this is your car!"

I was speechless and wondered how the expression on my face looked. "You mean this car is mine?"

"Yes, this car is yours. Do you like it?"

"I like it very much, because it will be the first car I ever had in my life. Thank you, you are so good to us, how can I ever repay you?"

"You don't have to, this is a gift for you and my boy."

Michael was all excited. He ran over to some kids playing outside and shouted, "Look you guys, my grandpa got us a car. Come and check it out!"

Opi was smiling as he said to me, "Look at him, he already sounds like an American boy."

"Yes," he sure does." I was very excited when I opened the car door.

Michael was the first one inside, "Let's go Mommy, hurry, let's go!"

We went for a ride through town and then on the freeway. I couldn't believe it; I was driving in my own car. It was baby blue with a black top. When we got home, I gave Opi a big hug and said, "Thank you very much, today is a very special day."

CHAPTER XII

I Pledge Allegiance to the Flag of The United States

Time passed, Michael went to school, I had my job, my English improved, and my confidence grew. We celebrated the American holidays and lived the American life style, "Life in the fast lane." Of course I kept some German traditions and spoke German at home so Michael wouldn't forget it. Living the American way was so much different from the East German way.

One example that I recall was the rules about eating times. In Germany, life was very military-like and regimented. Breakfast was around 7 a.m., lunch around noon, coffee and cake at 3 p.m., and dinner at 6 p.m. I noticed that in America it was so different; people ate when they were hungry. After awhile I began to eat this way, I liked it better.

We struggled from the beginning, but it was worth it, I never felt sorry or regret in making my choice, because it was for the better. I tried to find a job at what I knew best, as a glass engraver and designer. The only places I found for this type of work were in New York and Florida but we had just started getting comfortable living in Southern California, a wonderful place to live. A little shaky sometimes but nothing is perfect in this world. So I ended up in the electronics business; it was just a job to make a living.

I applied for United States' citizenship, another big step. This was one of my big goals when I planned on coming here. If I lived in this country I wanted to be a citizen and do things the American way, fitting in with society. After waiting many years, I went to the immigration service in Los Angeles and passed the test on my first attempt. I was so proud of myself!

Several months later, a letter arrived telling me the place and time for the citizenship swearing-in ceremony. I was excited and nervous. I dressed nicely because on that special day I wanted to look my best. I drove to Los Angeles to the Convention Center where the event took place. There were many people from different nations, all there for the same reason. I was to become an American citizen. It was always my dream, now the moment was so close. My legs trembled and felt like jelly.

A man behind a desk said, "Mama, I need to ask you for your green card. You don't need it anymore, congratulations!"

With a shaky voice I said, "Thank you sir, that's the nicest thing anyone has ever asked me to do. I will be a good citizen, I promise."

As the crowd pushed me into the hall, my heart started racing. Everybody had an American Flag, and a Judge swore us all in after the National Anthem was played. "You are not Irish, Polish, Russian, German, or Chinese, you are now an American, congratulations!" This was such a powerful moment for me, I felt like I was losing the ground under my feet, and cried tears of joy.

After I picked up my certificate, I went to my car and cried like a baby. That was December 12th, 1986 on my Mama's birthday; a day I will never forget. Now I was an American, as proud as I could be, with an indescribable feeling in my heart. I wished my Mama could have been there to celebrate with us; she would have been very happy. After I calmed down, my eyes were blurry from crying so much and my body was weak. I rested in the car for about 30 minutes before I returned home.

When I came home exhausted, Opi came over with a bottle of champagne. He gave me a hug and asked, "How does it feel to be an American?

Congratulations! Gitta, would you like to know why the East German government agreed with the Americans to let you and Michael leave the country?"

"Because of your help."

"Yes, that's true, I was part of it. *But believe it or not, I was told you were traded for modern computers.*"

I couldn't believe it, "are you serious?"

"Yes, very much so. And by the way, I brought you a present, I hope you like it."

When I opened it, I saw a big flag with the stars and stripes on it; I began to cry again. I found a special place for it, and everyday I looked at the beautiful flag and said, "God bless America." We grew older together and after thirty years Old Glory is still standing by my side. Besides the big one, I have many little flags all over the place, so I could always see them. They are a reminder of my first steps on American soil and a symbol of American freedom and power.

What an unforgettable day that was in my life, I was so proud to become an American. When he was thirteen Michael automatically became a citizen too.

The Fall of the Berlin Wall

One day I checked the calendar, and I noticed that my cat Schatzi needed shots. The vet was a nice young man. We had known each other for some time.

After he took care of my cat, he came back all excited and said, "Come into my office, you're not going to believe what just happened."

I got nervous; I thought he was talking about my cat. "Where is Schatzei, is she okay?"

"Yes, she is okay, just listen to the radio."

I heard people shouting and screaming, it sounded like a big celebration, but I didn't know what it was about. I heard the reporter say, "The Berlin Wall went down." I felt like a big piece of this 12-foot high wall had fallen on me. The unthinkable had just happened. This did not seem real, because everyone believed that this day would never come. I was shocked and almost ran out the door without my cat.

The vet called me back and said, "Don't forget your cat." He knew my story and understood what It meant to me.

I couldn't get home fast enough to watch TV.

Opi came with a friend and a champagne bottle, and was shouting, "Did you hear Gitta? The wall just came down."

I was so numb I couldn't talk; my chest hurt and tears ran down my chin. I remembered what President Ronald Regan said in his speech, "Mr. Gorbachev, tear down that wall!" It was unbelievable. This was the end of living behind the Iron Curtain. It meant freedom for millions of Germans. After twenty-eight years, Germany was reunified again, but it wouldn't have been possible without the help of America. This day, *November 9th 1989*, would forever be part of history. I was happy for all of the people because I knew what life under communism was like. One big piece of this wall is at the Regan library, standing as a memorial to this moment.

My son, Michael, I call him Mike, got his first surfboard at the age of twelve. We both loved the ocean and would spend most of our weekends at this beautiful place. He taught himself how to surf and became very good at it. Many times my car was loaded with his friends and all of their surfboards. We lived only twenty minutes away from the ocean and it was a great way to relax and be lazy. It felt so good feeling the warm sun on my skin; the smell of the ocean, sound of the waves, watching the surfers, the dolphins, the boats, and people walking by. The palm trees waved in the breeze and I thought to myself, "It can't be better than this, it is paradise." I am sure that there are many nice places on this earth that I have never seen, but for me Southern California is the best.

When Michael turned sixteen, he grew to be a handsome young man, an American boy. He had many friends, most of them from rich parents. They all liked to hang out at our apartment, and would say to me, "I feel more comfortable here than in our own houses. They would always tell Mike "Your Mom is cool!"

Sometimes Mike would ask, "Mom I need new jeans and shoes."

"Okay, lets go to Kmart."

"Mom, my friends will make fun of me."

Whatever was in style was expensive and I couldn't afford to buy it. "Sorry Mike, but I have to make sure that I can pay the rent, bills and put food on the table. You have to understand that." I tried to keep him happy, but sometimes it wasn't easy.

Then Opi would take Mike shopping, he would say, "Let's go my boy, Opi will take you shopping." He bought him everything he wanted. One day before Christmas Opi came and said to me, "I would like to take the boy for a ride, if that's okay with you."

"It's okay with me." I wanted to wrap presents and put them under our small artificial tree. Several hours later they came back with big grins on their faces and a witty look. "What's the matter, what are you two up to?"

"Nothing, we're just being silly." Mike was excited and could not wait to tell me. "Mommy, Mommy, Opi got me a Christmas present. Guess what it is?"

"Let's see, maybe a jacket, shoes, new surfboard or wetsuit?"

"You guessed wrong, it's a car!"

"What do you mean a car, a remote control car?"

"No, wrong again Mom, it's in our parking lot."

I saw a white car.

He opened the door and said, "Come on Mom, I'll take you for a ride. I'm the chauffeur now. Remember, I just got my license."

I was speechless for a while and then I said to Opi, "I don't know, this is such an expensive present."

"Let me do this, I love the boy and he is such a good kid. He keeps me young, and look at how happy he is."

About eight months later Opi had a small stoke. "It's stress from the job," the doctor said. He was okay, but five months later another one struck him. After that he was not the same anymore. He still came to visit, but it was so sad to see him in this condition, without being able to help him.

"Opi, I don't think it's a good idea for you to drive anymore." I said that because he'd caused two accidents within a month. Luckily, no one was hurt, only the cars were damaged.

He became very angry with me and said, "What are you trying to tell me, that I'm sick and not a good driver? The hell with you." His brain wasn't functioning normally anymore and one day he asked, "I am going to Germany, would you two like to come with me?"

"I can't because I can't take off of work, and Mike can't miss school."
We didn't see or hear from him for a while until I got a birthday card from
Germany. His writing was bad, like he couldn't hold the pen. Not long after
that I received a letter dated June 17th that had a Black Cross on it; in Germany
this means that someone has died. That's how I learned the sad news. I
was told that he had another stroke, was brought to the hospital and died of
internal bleeding. I wondered how on the same day that his birthday card
was written and dated, he could have died. (The birthday card had arrived
two weeks prior to June 17th.) It remains a mystery to me even today. Maybe
this was his way of saying goodbye. It was a major loss for me and hit Michael
very hard. He was a good man with a big heart. He took us under his wings,
and did so much to help us. We still miss him very much. He always said he
wanted to be buried in his hometown. He got his wish and was laid to rest
next to his mother.

A Strange Phone Call

For us, the ones left behind, life has to go on. Mike had had jobs after
school since he was 13 years old. He graduated from high school, went to
junior college and then transferred to a California State University. We didn't
see each other too often, mostly on weekends. I helped him out when I
could, buying books, food and paying the rent. He was living with two other
students, sharing a house near the beach. It seemed like it would be an
ordinary Sunday, until around 9 a.m when the phone rang. When Michael was
in the middle of finals something unexpected happened. Even though I did
not want to disturb him, I did. This phone call would make a big difference
to our future. "Hello." There was no answer. I hung up. Ten minutes later
it rang again, but no one was on the other line. Crazy people, if you don't
want to talk, then don't call. Minutes later it rang again; I was beginning to
get angry. "Who is this? Leave me alone."

Then I heard someone with a German accent, "Are you Brigitte?"

"Who wants to know?"

"Is your mothers' name Christel?"

"This is none of your business what my mothers' name is." I was even
angrier, wanting to hang up the phone.

I heard the voice on the other side saying, "Brigitte, it's me Erica. I met
you at your mothers' house, and when you visited us we went on a boat ride
on the lake."

"Oh yes, now I remember. How are you and how is your husband?"

"Okay, we are okay. I apologize about the phone; I don't have your number or address. Friends of mine live in your area and they looked you up in the phone book."

Now it started to make sense to me and I asked, "What can I do for you, why have you called?"

"You need to come to Arizona immediately, because your mother just passed away."

The news took me by surprise. "What do you mean Arizona, I thought my mother lived in California?"

"She moved to Arizona, that's where I'm calling from. You have to come quickly to identify the body. Bring your birth certificate, I'll explain everything else later."

I had avoided seeing my Mother for the last several years; I dreaded the idea of having to identify her. I had no idea she was living in Arizona, it came as a surprise to me. I was afraid to see her and did not want to go there alone. I called Michael but nobody answered. I called repeatedly for several hours until he answered.

"Where have you been?"

"I was at the library studying for my finals. What's wrong Mom, you sound upset?"

I told him what happened and asked him to call the airport and make reservations to Phoenix. I'll come to your house and we'll leave from there together. If we go by car we won't make it in time."

"But Mom, I am in the middle of finals."

"I know son, we will take care of that later."

At that time, I was working lots of overtime on a big contract my company had. Nobody was allowed to take time off, but in my case it was an emergency situation. When we arrived in Phoenix we had to board another plane to Tucson, where my Mother died.

I was very nervous. Michael, "I just pray to God that I don't have to see her."

We ran around in the hospital looking for the doctor who signed the death certificate, but he wasn't on duty that day. Then another doctor said, "It's not necessary, someone has already identified her. From there we had to go to a funeral home to make arrangements for her cremation. I didn't have answers to the mortician's questions, so I called Erica for help. "After you're done, rent a car and come to my house," she said. She gave us directions and after about two hours we arrived in a small town in the desert. "Look at you, Michael, you're so handsome and tall. The last time I saw you you were just a little boy. And how well you speak German!"

"My Mom made sure I wouldn't forget."

She told me the whole story and at the end she said, "I've already made an appointment with a lawyer. We have to be there by 10 a.m. tomorrow morning." Then she held me and looked me in the eye and said with a smile, "You will get everything your mother had, because she didn't make a will."

I didn't know what to say and asked Erica to come with us because she knew her better than I.

"Lets go to her place," which was just a few minutes away from Erica's house. Then she gave me a key. "Now when you open the door, everything you see is all yours; there's even money in the bank."

I felt sick and said, "Excuse me, I think I have to throw up," and went straight to the bathroom. She had bought a brand new five-bedroom mobile home. The next morning we headed to the lawyers office. An old man with a cowboy hat was sitting behind the desk. I told him that we had to be back in California by the weekend because of Michael's school and my job.

"I don't think I can finish everything by that time, you'll have to come back."

Erica sat behind us and listened, she then spoke with the lawyer to see if the work could be finished earlier. He went with us to city hall and a few other places, then to the bank to close out the account. He said that the laws were different than in California, and he would pull some strings to speed things up.

I was very thankful for that. We started packing and making arrangements for a moving truck with trailer, for her belongings and car. We decided to sell her home and drive back to California with our new possessions.

When we started packing I said to Erica, "I don't know, this does not feel right to me, it's like I robbed her house."

"Don't be stupid and think this way, your mother never did anything for you or Michael. Don't feel badly, you deserve all this.

The truck was loaded to the top and the car was loaded onto the trailer. We left so much stuff behind, some for Erica and other neighbors who helped. In all of the rush, Mike hurt his wrist doing some heavy lifting. It was swollen, red and he was in lots of pain. Mike asked me to drive the truck because of his arm. I was a nervous wreck, and said to him, "I can't Mike, I'm too nervous we'll crash. "I've never driven anything that big."

"Nether have I," Mike said. Fearing for our safety, I didn't even try to drive. Mike agreed to drive the truck.

I wasn't in good shape. In all of my hurry, I had forgotten my medication. My feet were swollen and burned like fire. In addition to that I was also suffering from the heat and the reality of the situation.

There was always one question that I had never asked my mother, "Why couldn't you be a mother to me?" and now the answer was blowing in the hot desert wind.

After several hours Michael said, "Mom, I can't drive much longer, my arm is in a lot of pain."

I felt badly. He was in a tough situation and I couldn't help him. At the next gas station I got some ice and aspirin for him. We drove the entire day, stopping only for gas. We finally arrived in San Diego and then on to Los Angeles. Once we got there, we met a large traffic jam.

"Oh my god, this is all we need," and I reached for a cigarette.

"Mom, give me one too."

I was surprised. "I didn't think you smoked."

"I don't, I just need something to numb me."

After so many hours of driving, we came home completely exhausted.

"What a trip."

"I'll never forget this one," Mike said.

"Neither will I."

The whole week was very stressful for us, not to mention the desert heat. The next day Michael went to see a doctor; he had a pulled muscle. He went back to school and still did well on his finals.

After being back home the reality of what had happened hit me. All the stuff I got, the money and the car, was starting to sink in. I wanted to buy a house but didn't have enough money because housing was very expensive in Southern California. Instead, I ended up buying a mobile home. I found a big one with a fireplace, just a few minutes from the apartments where I used to live. What an exciting day it was, the day I opened the door to my own home. I felt like a queen who had moved into her castle.

Michael gave me a big hug and said, *You deserve all of this Mom, I'm so happy for you and I love you very much!"*

LIFE is FULL of SURPRISES

One evening I cleaned up the kitchen after dinner. It was after 6 p.m. and the phone rang. A man on the other end asked if I was Brigitte. Not recognizing the voice I asked, "Who would like to know?"

"I have three gentleman in my taxi. They're from Germany and would like to see you."

I thought of who it could possibly be.

Then the taxi driver said, "One moment please, one of them would like to talk to you."

I heard a man saying in German, "Do you remember me? I am Doctor Messer."

I almost dropped the phone, because the surgeon who operated on me 24 years ago was also a Dr. Messer. It's funny, because his name Messer means knife in German. If this was the same doctor how could he still remember me all these years?

"The taxi driver helped us find your phone number. I'm in Los Angeles with two friends and we would like to see you if that's okay."

To make sure this was the same doctor I used to know, I asked, "Are you Dr. Klaus Messer?"

"Yes, that's me!"

"Oh my god, what a surprise. This is unbelievable, yes of course, please come and see me."

I was very excited as I gave the taxi driver directions to my house. About forty minutes later, the doorbell rang and with a pounding heartbeat I rushed to the door. There he stood, in person, with a smile. He gave me a big hug and flowers. After I welcomed him and his two friends he introduced me to his colleagues. One of them was Dr. Keunzel, a biologist, and the tall one a Professor Dr. Steinhausen, an expert in cancer research. From our conversation I found out that they were in Los Angeles for a medical convention.

I asked Dr. Messer, "How is it that you still remember me?"

"Very simple. When you left East Germany, everybody talked about you and you were also my patient." With a smile he said, "Some I will never forget."

I was a little embarrassed and said; "To have you here in my house is really something special for me!" I opened a bottle of champagne. "Today is a special day with special people, and that is a reason to celebrate." When I saw these educated and well-spoken gentleman, I felt so small, but I also realized how down-to-earth they were. We had so much to talk about their lives and mine. We discussed Dr. Messer's brother who was also a doctor. About two years before I left East Germany, he had escaped with his whole family to the west. His wife hung laundry in the garden; the TV and all the lights were on in order to make people think they were home. They left everything behind and the next morning they had vanished. The government kept a special eye on the educated people; it needed them and didn't want to lose them after paying for their education. I still remember when the news got around, and Dr. Klaus Messer was being watched to make sure he didn't leave.

Time flew and when I heard the horn from the taxi, it was time to say farewell. I thanked them for coming and wished them a safe flight to Germany. What a big surprise it was, it made my day and many more to come. Since then, we have not seen each other, but for me it was an event which I will never forget. It was nice to know that there was someone somewhere in this big world who remembered me. It was something I would always appreciate.

Chapter XIII

A New Sunrise

L ife guides us in many different directions. Sometimes it makes us climb mountains or walk on an endless, bumpy road. It's like riding on a roller coaster with ups and downs; with rainy and sunny days.

When situations went from bad to worse, I was always optimistic because my Momma used to say to me, "Look at the sky Gitta, behind the dark clouds is a star shining just for you."

I never forgot her saying those words to me, and all through my life I believed in my hopes and dreams and reached for that star. How often I looked at the sky for that special one. And many years later, I found it; clear, bright, shining and sparkling like a diamond in the sky. I knew my Mama was looking out for me in her own unique way. By sending this star to me all of my problems fell away. This was my Mama. I could always count on her because she had never let me down.

Michael and I are very fortunate; our lives changed for the better. He grew up to be a tall and handsome young man. He went to college, got his undergraduate degree, and years later his Masters' degree. From the time he was a little boy, his passion was cars and naturally he has worked in the automotive business ever since.

He has often said, "Mom, thank you for raising me the way you did. I wouldn't be the person I am without you, and thank you for bringing me to America."

Hearing these words from him means much to me and I know I did something right. Raising my son was always the first priority to me. This was the biggest role of my life. Being a loving and caring mother, I accomplished the promise that I had made to myself. Most of the time it was not easy being a single parent in a strange world, but like my Mama used to say, "There is always a shining star behind every dark cloud." After many bad things happened something good will come out of it, and I found it.

After running from the past and as time went by, I realized that some of my wounds had healed but the scars would always remain. Now I am retired and live everyday as it is my last because we never know what will happen. I thank God every day for letting me wake up to see the sunshine again. My life was always a simple one and I appreciated the little things; taking nothing for granted and being grateful for his blessings. Most of all I am glad to have seen Michael grow up in a better world than I did.

America, What a Country!

Now I have a part time job taking care of the elderly and working in my garden. Besides that, I have two cats and a dog that I rescued before they were put to sleep. I'm just like my Mama, I can't sit still, but as we know, staying physically and mentally active keeps one in good shape. I've stayed in touch with friends in Germany and send money to them to put flowers on Mama's grave on her birthday. One of these days I would love to go back with roses for Mama, her favorite flower. I have many things I want to tell her; to let her know how much I love her, and that one day we will be united again.

It's a turn of life; people come into this world and one day will go out. My family loved ones who were close to me are no longer here. I'm the only survivor, but my day too will come. It's a good thing we don't know when it will because we would all be crazy, very confused. The fact is, we're all in the same boat. There's a higher power that we can't control, just trust.

We are all on this earth for the same reason, to live and to die. I could never understand why people can't live together in peace and harmony. We have to respect each other without hate and prejudice and prevent our lives from being cut short by violence and war. In doing so this world would be a better place. But no matter how brutal it can be living thru the dark days, if we give up we will never discover how precious life can be. For me it was a walk on a long bumpy road with many obstacles and challenges along the way; a road from hell to heaven.

Now, 65 years later my life story is coming to a happy ending. When I look back, I realize how the times and people have changed over many years, and will continue to change as long as the world turns. Did I have a good life? I will let you be the judge. One thing I know is that everything that happened made me a stronger and more tolerant person.

Thank you America, for letting Michael and me be a part of this beautiful country, thank you for listening to my story. From the bottom of our hearts we would like to say, "We are very proud to be American, God Bless America, God Bless you all."

Michael and I were sitting on the beach as he read the hand-written copy of my story. The sunset disappeared into the ocean like a big ball of fire and the water glittered golden. We could smell the ocean and feel a soft touch on our skin from the breeze. We had a nice conversation and enjoyed our surroundings; it was just an ordinary California day.

After a moment of silence Michael said, "Wow mom, that's an emotional story! I had no idea that you have been through so much, especially as a little girl. It's amazing that you are such a wonderful person after all that you have endured. I feel very lucky to have been raised by you. Do you see the houses behind us? That's where the rich and famous live."

"I know son, we have seen many of them in person. I feel rich as well, just being here and having you by my side. I feel like I am sitting in a big sandbox full of diamonds, and you are the most valuable one of them all."

"I love you Mom."

"I love you too son."